This is the stuff you've always been embarrassed to ask about the world of modern business.

The *What You Need to Know . . .* books can get you up to speed on a core business subject fast. Whether it's for a new job, a new responsibility, or a meeting with someone you need to impress, these books will give you what you need to get by as someone who knows what they're talking about.

Each book contains:

> ▶ **What It's all About** – a summary of key points
> ▶ **Who You Need to Know** – the basics about the key players
> ▶ **Who Said It** – quotes from key figures
> ▶ **What You Need to Read** – books and online resources for if you want to deepen your knowledge
> ▶ **If You Only Remember One Thing** – a one-liner of the most important information

You might also want to know:

> ▶ *What You Need to Know about Business*
> ▶ *What You Need to Know about Economics*
> ▶ *What You Need to Know about Project Management*
> ▶ *What You Need to Know about Strategy*
> ▶ *What You Need to Know about Leadership*
> ▶ *What You Need to Know about Starting a Business*

WHAT YOU NEED TO KNOW ABOUT MARKETING

SIMON MIDDLETON

CAPSTONE

Registered office
Capstone Publishing Ltd. (A Wiley Company), The Atrium, Southern
Gate, Chichester, West Sussex, PO19 8SQ, United Kingdom

For details of our global editorial offices, for customer services and for
information about how to apply for permission to reuse the copyright
material in this book please see our website at www.wiley.com.

Library of Congress Cataloguing-in-Publication Data

9780857081506 (paperback), 9780857081704 (epub),
9780857081711 (emobi), ISBN 9781119974881 (ebk)

A catalogue record for this book is available from the British Library.

Set in 10.5 on 13.5 New Baskerville by Toppan Best-set Premedia Limited

Printed in Great Britain by TJ International Ltd., Padstow, Cornwall

CONTENTS

INTRODUCTION

I have a good friend who hates marketing. She thinks it's of dubious morality and questionable effectiveness. Actually, she thinks marketing is 'rubbish'. Well that's not the word she uses, but you get the idea.

It's hardly surprising she feels this way. And she's not alone. Marketing has a bad reputation. Worse still it has a hugely confused and confusing one. It is often considered to be synonymous with 'spin' or 'manipulation' (bad things and the work of evil geniuses in the view of its opponents). Equally it is often dismissed as stuff and nonsense (and therefore condemned as the work of fools who aren't capable of doing proper jobs).

Evil genius or pointless nonsense? They can't both be true. Can they?

In fact marketing is probably one of the earliest activities ever undertaken by mankind, after hunting, making fire and building shelter. Because marketing, when you get right down to it, is based on the simple idea of exchange between people.

I have some fresh meat because I spent my day hunting. You have sharper tools than me because you spent your day flint-knapping. If I give you a leg of my deer, will you give me one of your stone knives so I can skin the beast? Fair exchange is no robbery, as we may well have grunted to each other back then. That's exchange, the swapping of something of value for something of roughly (estimated, negotiated and agreed) equal value.

That's not marketing in its totality of course, but it is the heart of the matter. One cave dweller approaching another with the 'deer-leg for flint knife' proposition is marketing, albeit of a primitive sort. The initiator with the fresh deer in this case is the marketer, and the flint-knapper is the customer. Although it could have been the other way round. Take this thought experiment a little further. Our deer hunter discovers a real talent for catching deer and offers to specialise in this, 'trading' the resulting abundance of fresh meat with others in the clan, in exchange for gathered fruit, or arrows, or some paint for the cave walls! Suddenly we've got a small business. A business which has relationships with customers. And the word that most accurately describes those relationships is: marketing.

Because fundamentally marketing is about relationships. And if we flash forward a few millennia to the present day, when marketing is more sophisticated than it has ever been before, we discover that marketing is still about relationships, and that marketing still lies at the very centre of this human activity that we call business.

Of course if we didn't need or want to exchange (to do business with each other) then we wouldn't need to do marketing. And you wouldn't need to read this book. But the reverse is also true. If we don't do marketing, then we can't do business. Or to put it more bluntly: if we don't understand marketing and do it well, then our businesses (or our charity, or even our public sector organisation) will under-perform, perhaps to the point of going under. And the sad truth is that many businesses don't do marketing well, at all.

We live and work and trade in challenging times. Too many businesses are focused on every aspect of what they do (from technology to cost cutting) apart from the one which could make such a huge difference to their fortunes: their marketing.

This book isn't a history of marketing, or a philosophical exploration of marketing. Neither is it a detailed action plan which will solve all your marketing problems for you. This book tells you what you really *need* to know about marketing: and it assumes, to be on the safe side, that you may not have known very much about marketing before you picked it up. If you only ever read one book about the subject, then if it's this one you'll have the essential concepts to help you to understand and ultimately to 'do' marketing better (or at least to contribute to its being done by someone else in your company or organisation).

A final point before we begin: although I refer repeatedly in this book to companies and businesses, don't let this put you off if you work in a charity or a public sector organisation. The essential truths and concepts of marketing are equally applicable in the private, public and voluntary sectors, just as they are to organisations ranging in size from one person and his dog through to global super companies.

LET'S GET STARTED

WHO SAID IT . . .

"Marketing is managing profitable customer relationships."
– **Philip Kotler**

The absolute, number one, most important, and sacrosanct principle of marketing is that it's about customers. CUSTOMERS! That really can't be stressed enough, because so many people think that marketing is either synonymous with sales, or is primarily concerned with advertising or other promotional activity. But it isn't: it's about customers, and to be even more specific it's about *relationships* with customers. To go back briefly to our cave dwellers: it's the relationship between them (which leads to the agreement between them) that is the really important part of the deal, rather than the deer leg or the stone tool in themselves. The point behind this is that marketing is not actually about selling as such but about fulfilling and satisfying the needs of your customer.

MARKETING VERSUS SALES

We need to clarify this marketing v. sales issue. Marketing and sales are not the same thing. But they still get confused. There are still quite substantial companies which have a senior person called 'Sales & Marketing Director', although it's less prevalent than even a decade ago. And why is it so important to stress that marketing and sales are fundamentally different from each other? Because marketing begins with what customers need and want, and sales begins with what the company needs to sell (because, for whatever reason, it's made a particular product and has lots of it, or it has designed a particular service and now needs to get that service picked up by customers). See the difference?

A restaurateur who owns three popular establishments told me once to always avoid choosing from the 'specials' board in unfamiliar restaurants. Why? Because, in the view of this particular insider at least, the specials board is about shifting whatever the restaurant has got slightly too much of in the larder. Lobster on the specials board? They've got a couple that didn't get ordered by customers yesterday and they absolutely have to use them today. The specials board therefore isn't marketing, because it's not about us, the customer. It is instead selling, because it's about them, the restaurant.

WHO SAID IT . . .

"The aim of marketing is to make
selling unnecessary."
– Peter Drucker

NEEDS VERSUS WANTS

To look at this another way, successful companies increasingly seem to be those who understand what real people
actually need and want (we'll explore the difference
between needs and wants presently) and then do something to fulfil that need or want. Less successful (and
failing companies) have a tendency to be those who produced or provided whatever they wanted to produce or
provide (or whatever they had always produced or provided) rather then paying heed to what customers might
want to buy. There's a caveat to this statement of course
(and it won't be the last caveat in this book) which is that
paying heed to customer needs and wants IS NOT THE
SAME as assuming that the customers always know in
advance what they need and want.

Before the iPod we didn't know we wanted one did we? Go back further. Before the Sony Walkman (if you're old enough to remember the excitement of this device arriving in 1981 like a vision of the future in those dark days), we didn't really know that we needed or wanted a cassette recorder that we could clip to our belts and listen to with headphones. Still less a cassette recorder that didn't actually record but only played back. And of course the Walkman, and subsequently the iPod, were not only huge commercial successes, but also cultural and market game-changers.

So don't fall into the trap of thinking that customers know everything, especially in advance of the fact. They don't. But that doesn't make Sony or Apple reckless anti-marketers. Far from it. Sony geeks took their proto-device (which was not backed initially by the corporation) onto the Tokyo underground system and used it. It wasn't long before they had gathered strong evidence that there was a 'market' for the device. The rest is history. And it is a history which directly informed Apple in their development of the iPod. The 'market' for the mobile music device was already proven. Apple took it into the digital era.

If you think about it, Apple has never really had to 'sell' us the iPod, or any of its other devices (at least not since its reinvention as a marketing-oriented company, with the launch of the iMac in the early 1990s). Apple certainly does advertising, and high-profile advertising too, and it spends huge sums on communications of many different kinds. But it doesn't have to persuade us to buy. Instead it creates a scenario in which enough of us are passionately keen to do so. See the difference?

So, marketing is much misunderstood and sometimes maligned. Yet its role in the modern economy, and in the survival and prosperity of virtually any business, large or small, is indisputable. Some claim marketing is a science. Others would call it an art. It is perhaps more appropriate to describe it as a mindset, or an outlook.

The intention of this book is to show that this marketing mindset is not only critical to business success, but also exciting in itself, both to understand and to engage in.

To enjoy and find value in this book you don't need to have any prior marketing knowledge at all. It will take you through all the key concepts in marketing, from its origins as a discipline through to the very latest 'digital' thinking.

The book covers the fundamental building blocks of marketing: looking at the 'big ideas' about customers and markets, products and services, pricing, promotion and distribution. Along the way you'll meet most of the great marketing thinkers, including some names who will be very familiar (but whom you may not have thought of as marketers).

Each chapter also provides key pointers for further reading, both offline and online, to take exploration of particular concepts further if you wish.

This book isn't intended to turn anyone into a marketer overnight: but it will enable you to understand your marketing specialist colleagues (not to mention helping you to cut through the jargon), and will put you in a very strong position to make a persuasive case for a marketing mindset in your company or organisation.

CHAPTER 1

THE CUSTOMERS

WHAT IT'S ALL ABOUT

- ► The difference between needs, wants and demands
- ► Value propositions and marketing offers
- ► Giving customers sufficient value to make them 'satisfied'
- ► Building customer relationships

Arguably the most important fundamental concepts in marketing are those of *needs* and *wants*: the prime motivators for the human behaviour which turns us into 'customers'. Without needs and wants there would be no motivation for us to buy. The marketer's first task therefore is to consider what it is that people actually need and want, even if those people don't yet know the answer themselves.

NEEDS, WANTS AND DEMANDS

A self-assured female character in a well-known Bob Dylan song points out to her hesitant lover that whilst his debutante girlfriend might well know what he 'needs', it is she that knows what he actually 'wants'. We know exactly what is being implied here and it points up an important concept in marketing: the difference between needs, wants and demands.

Our needs can be described as things that are fundamental to us as humans. Fundamental, but not necessarily physical. We need air, water, food. We need to be out of the cold, and out of the scorching sun. We need protection from danger. But we need more than those physical and environmental basics. We need to be part of social groups. We need a sense of 'security' which goes beyond immediate safety. And we seem, as humans, to have a need to understand what is going on in our world. From primitive reassurance that the sun will rise tomorrow, through to more sophisticated under-standing about 'why' (embracing science, religion, philosophy).

The famous hierarchy of needs described by Abraham Maslow is still hard to beat as a summary of our multi-layered human needs. Maslow's model is useful and descriptive, but some contemporary thinkers point out that it is also limited in outlook, in that it is hierarchical. Maslow argued in this model that we only feel, express, and seek to satisfy our 'higher needs' once we have ful-filled the more basic ones. His critics say this is wrong: and that even those people for whom the finding of food, shelter and safety are daily challenges nevertheless have higher needs at the same time. Interestingly, it is remarked by some commentators that Maslow said before his death that he regretted the hierarchical nature of his model and acknowledged that humans strive for higher meanings and for 'self-actualisation' even when they are otherwise at the bottom of his notional pyramid, where they are also struggling daily for the bare essentials to stay alive. Notwithstanding that revision of the concept, it remains a useful model for considering the kinds of needs that humans have.

WHO YOU NEED TO KNOW
Abraham Maslow

Not a marketer at all, but highly influential on marketing primarily because of his Hierarchy of Needs model and his theory of self-actualisation. Abraham Maslow (1908–1970) was a Russian émigré raised in Brooklyn, New York. In the 1950s he was one of the founding thinkers of the school of humanistic psychology, which focused on human potential and personal growth: aspects of psychology intrinsically attractive to marketers. Maslow's hierarchy model suggests that people seek to meet basic physiological needs like food, water, warmth and sleep before they move on to higher level needs. Further up the hierarchy, usually visualised as a pyramid, are 'higher' needs including personal esteem, accomplishment, and ultimately self-actualisation. The model has obvious implications for marketers, although many would now dispute its basic premise and argue that humans are capable and driven to seek higher needs simultaneously to dealing with the lower ones.

Maslow's hierarchy of needs

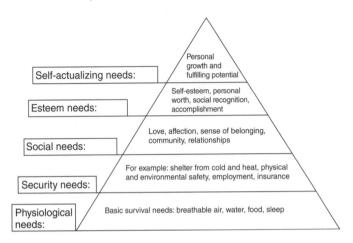

The real significance of needs though is that they are unavoidable. As the cliché goes, there will always be a market for undertakers. Meeting needs is the basis of so much of our economic activity of course. From building houses to baking bread, from growing potatoes to making shoes.

But meeting needs is far from the only way to go to market. Because we don't just need: we also want!

If our needs are unavoidable, then at least they are relatively limited. Maslow encapsulated them fairly simply. Our wants on the other hand are discretionary (in other words we can live without them), but they are also virtually unlimited and unpredictable in scope. They are also of course very often deeply irrational.

If you listen to teenagers talking in a shopping mall you'll hear the 'need' word used in an interesting way. One teenage girl shopper will point at a shop window display and say excitedly to her friends: 'Oh my God, I soooo need that top.'

She doesn't *need* that particular top of course. At least not in a way that could be described in purely rational (or in Maslow's) terms. No, she doesn't need to buy it, but she certainly *wants* to do so. 'Wants' may not be as old as needs in the scheme of things, but they aren't far behind, and they have long been rich territory for marketers and arguably the key driver of what we refer to as 'the consumer society'.

WHO SAID IT . . .

"Yes, I sell people things they don't need. I can't, however, sell them something they don't want. Even with advertising."
– John E. O'Toole

Because we have needs and wants we also have the environment in which exchange, business and thus marketing can take place. And the marketer in any given company or organisation should be primarily engaged in understanding those needs and wants and steering their company towards the satisfaction of them.

But there is a third dimension which has to be considered, the pinnacle of the needs/wants model: *demands*. Demands are simply wants which are backed by sufficient buying power to make them unavoidable by the marketer.

There was a time when we did most of our banking by visiting a branch on our high street or in our village or neighbourhood. First Direct pioneered the use of phone banking in the UK, more than 20 years ago. First Direct appealed then to the 'wants' of a relatively small number of customers interested in a new approach to banking, unrestricted by the need to be physically present or by the opening times of high street banks. Not many years later, having been copied in their phone banking offering by most other banks (although less effectively by most), First Direct was one of a new set of banking pioneers focusing on using the internet as the prime interface between bank and customer.

Now of course that early 'want' of a few people (usually referred to as early-adopters) for phone and internet banking has become a 'demand' of many. Very few banking customers in the developed economies would consider choosing a new bank which didn't provide

24-hour phone and internet banking. There are exceptions to this (there are always exceptions in marketing), such as certain private banks, or customers (mainly older) for whom the phone and internet services are much less relevant and appealing (they don't want them).

There is a downside to this example of demand in action. Smaller bank branches are being closed as the big providers consolidate their high street presence, keeping their staff costs low as they continue to develop their internet services. One result is that older people, like my 91 year-old Mum for example, is faced with the imminent prospect of her much-valued local branch closing down. It's not that my Mum doesn't want this branch. She does. The point is that she cannot 'demand' it, because she (even if she along with all her friends of a similar age all marched into the branch in protest at its closure) do not represent sufficient buying power.

Demands are therefore simply wants that are backed with the muscle of buying power!

WHO YOU NEED TO KNOW
Philip Kotler

Widely acknowledged as the world's leading expert on strategic marketing practice, Dr. Philip Kotler has become the 'guru of gurus' in the field. Kotler, born in 1931, is the author of the definitive marketing textbook *Marketing Management*, currently in its 13th edition. He teaches all over the world and his consultancy firm Kotler Marketing Group advises some of the world's leading brands. Kotler's work is so wide ranging and extensive that it is impossible to sum up in a few lines, but his core and most influential idea could be said to be that the discipline of marketing is fundamentally about the creation of value for customers. Coupled with that concept is his observation that the world economic landscape is forever and massively altered by technology and by globalisation. Kotler describes the phenomenon of 'hyper-competition', referring to the ability of companies to produce far more than can be sold, thus putting huge pressure on price but also creating a greater need than ever before for constant innovation and the creation of 'perceived' differentiation. The power, says Kotler, has passed irrevocably to the customer.
'The customer is King'.

VALUE PROPOSITIONS

When a company, in whatever field, sees that there are some potential customers out there who appear to need the product or service that they are skilled in providing, all they have to do is provide it, yes?

If only it were as simple as you (a paint manufacturer for example) spotting that some people do indeed like to paint things (their walls perhaps) and therefore confidently boosting your paint production. That'll work won't it? At least you are responding to a market need. Well, again, not quite.

Successful marketers tend to succeed not with a simple response to a perceived need or want (or even demand) but instead by creating what is known as a 'value proposition'. A value proposition just refers to creating a set of benefits which will fulfil the customer's need or want.

Let's unpick that a little. The word benefit is important. Being beneficial means that something or someone does something good for someone. A benefit in our sense therefore does something good for your customer. And if you look closely at almost any customer in almost any scenario you'll see that they are looking for something that does them some good, although the 'good' can vary.

WHO SAID IT . . .

"Authentic marketing is not the art of selling what you make but knowing what to make. It is the art of identifying and understanding customer needs and creating solutions that deliver satisfaction to the customers, profits to the producers and benefits for the stakeholders."
– Philip Kotler

One customer may be on a really tight budget, with minimal cash, but they want to cheer up the walls of their child's bedroom or their kitchen. There's the benefit they're after, right there: cheery and refreshed rooms with absolute minimum negative impact on their purse. Do you have a value proposition for them (a low-cost range of basic but appealing colours)?

Another customer is looking for traditional hues and very high quality coverage to suit their painstakingly restored Georgian town house. Do you have a value proposition for them (a much wider range of subtler shade variations in a quality paint which is as close possible in look and feel to the coverings of 200 years ago)?

Neither of these customers is better or worse than the other. And you might serve either one or both very profitably. But you won't achieve that by just making paint. No, you have to create the set of benefits which will meet and fulfil their specific needs or wants. That's your 'value proposition'.

MARKETING OFFERS

And once the value proposition (benefits that meet wants and needs) is created, is the job done? Sorry, not just yet. You know the old saying about building a better mousetrap and having the world beat a path to your door? It's usually attributed to Ralph Waldo Emerson. Actually he didn't say exactly that. What he wrote was fuller and more interesting, and seductive . . . but still wrong. Emerson actually wrote:

'If a man has good corn or wood, or boards, or pigs, to sell, or can make better chairs or knives, crucibles or church organs than anybody else, you will find a broad hard-beaten road to his house, though it be in the woods.'

Emerson's statement is enormously appealing. It plays to the producer in us: the farmer, the craftsman, the creator. All of Emerson's examples (except for church organs) can be considered needs, and staple needs at that. Folk will always need food, building materials, furniture to sit on. But attractive as it is, this outlook is dangerously misleading. It is in effect the opposite of marketing, but it's a position (a mousetrap if you like) that many companies, both large and small, walk right into and find themselves stuck in. Why? Because it leaves the *customer* out of the equation.

Building a better chair, for example, is a wonderful thing, provided that the amount of time you spent perfecting it, and the cost of the superior materials, do not make the selling price of this king of chairs prohibitive for your neighbours who are predisposed to buy chairs. Unless of course you happen to know that in the not too distant town there are more genteel and affluent folk who can and will pay a premium for your excellent furniture. Aha, you think, they have a need for chairs (we all do) and a want for really nice chairs such as mine! And you have a heck of a value proposition for them (superior hand-crafted chairs with a rustic touch). But what is going to make these highly desirable high-spending customers beat a path to your door? Well you can be certain that the value proposition alone won't do the trick.

No, what you need next is a 'marketing offer'. The marketing offer is what brings the value proposition to life in a way that is relevant to your prospective customer. There are numerous elements to a marketing offer, but in essence it is this: the collection and combination of your product or your service (often both), plus the information you create and provide about it, plus the actual 'experience' of learning about, buying and using the product or service. In other words the marketing offer is the whole shooting match, the entire customer experience (tangible, financial, verbal, visual, behavioural, emotional).

The marketing offer therefore embraces the value proposition but goes way beyond it. And that gives another handy description of marketing and its fundamental and unique character. Marketing begins long before the product exists, and it goes on long after the sale is made. Marketing thus embraces production as well as sales.

When it comes right down to it, you can build the best mousetrap that the world has ever known and you can protect it with patents and trademarks to your heart's content. But unless you create first a value proposition that meets the needs and wants of your customers, and then a marketing offer that 'speaks' to them, you ain't going to make any money. And as you often hear the investors of *Dragon's Den* say: that won't be a business, that will be a hobby.

Businesses that are focused on sales, or on production, rather than marketing, can become so fixated on the former aspects that they become blind to the latter: the really important thing, finding a solution or a fulfilment to customers' needs and wants.

Kotler puts this customer-centric view of marketing very simply and elegantly. There are five steps he says:

▶ First, understand the marketplace and the customer needs and wants.

▶ Second, design a customer-driven marketing strategy.

▶ Third, construct an integrated marketing programme that delivers superior value.

▶ Fourth, build profitable relationships and create customer delight

▶ Fifth, capture value in return from customers to create profits and customer equity

THE DIFFERENCE BETWEEN CUSTOMERS AND CONSUMERS

In all this talk of the importance of customers, we have to remember that there is an important difference between the concepts of the 'customer' and the 'consumer'. The child who goes into the sweetshop and buys and then eats the sweets is both customer and consumer. But customer (buyer) and consumer (user) are not always the same person, and the marketer has to consider both: which is why for example so many children's food products are advertised with apparent health benefits highlighted alongside fun aspects.

The same distinction (and sometime blurring) occurs in business-to-business marketing. The individual authorising the purchase of the photocopier or company car (customer) is unlikely to be the user (consumer). To whom should the marketer be talking? Well, both, as we will examine in due course.

CUSTOMERS AND PROFIT

An uncomfortable truth about customers is that not all of them are good for business. Anyone who has ever worked in retail or hospitality will recognise that a relatively small proportion of customers create a relatively large proportion of issues and problems, ranging from complaints to demands for extra product information, special variants and so on. As the old saying goes: 'the customer isn't always right but he/she is always the customer'. So the resource-sapping customer must of course be looked after. But the business, of whatever kind, has to consider whether this kind of customer is profitable to the business.

The question we have to ask, in relation to the resource these customers demand, is do they buy enough, pay enough, return enough, or recommend to others enough, in order to be profitable?

With that caveat in mind though we should also bear in mind that some apparently unprofitable customers are in fact worthwhile, either because they can be nurtured and educated, or because they represent the crossover into a new market which can itself become profitable if handled correctly. The important behaviour for marketers is to observe and analyse sufficiently in order to decide which customers are profitable now, and of those which aren't which may become so in the future.

CUSTOMER VALUE AND CUSTOMER SATISFACTION

When people buy stuff (products, services, or experiences) they make their purchasing decision based on their perception (either their actual understanding or their wild imagining) of the value they are going to receive in return for their money. But it's important to remember that perception is very far from always being rational.

'Customer value' is a measure of the difference between what the customer gains from using, owning or experiencing the purchase, and the cost of obtaining it. It's a measure of 'worth', but that worth is highly subjective, and indeed subject to any number of external and internal forces.

Picture this scene. A few weeks ago I stopped at a rural petrol station en route for an important meeting (well it seemed important at the time). After filling it up, the flippin' car wouldn't start again. It was clearly a battery problem. The garage had no one present who could help, but a local farmer offered to start my car with jump leads from his truck. This was a value proposition. I needed to get moving or I would miss my appointment.

And here's where customer value comes in to the mix. The farmer had my car working again in about two minutes.

> 'What do I owe you?' I said to the farmer.
> 'What have you got?' he replied.
> 'I've only got a twenty pound note on me,' I said.
> 'That'll do it,' he said.

You may think this was a high price for two minutes activity or not, but at that moment, in my particular situation, it was sound customer value. Had my need not been acute (in terms of time) then I could have called out my breakdown service and not paid anything (I already pay membership after all). But right there and then, my breakdown service could not have solved my problem quickly enough. Only the local guy with the jump leads could do that. That's customer value.

In fact the customer value here is quite complex: both tangible and intangible, logical, practical and also highly emotional (because solving the problem removed my rapidly escalating stress).

And on that particular day, for those few minutes, there was a marketing niche which the farmer filled by starting my car quickly, and this in turn led to 'customer satisfaction' (notwithstanding the £20 price). He promised value to me and delivered on it, thus creating a satisfied customer.

CREATING PROFITABLE RELATIONSHIPS

The next step in the marketing process, which couldn't happen in this particular case, but which can and should happen in any marketing-focused business, is to build on that satisfaction to create a long-term relationship. This time around we made a transaction, a satisfactory one-off exchange, and no further relationship could happen. But successful marketing businesses go an important extra step to create profitable relationships.

We all know, instinctively almost, that an existing customer is more valuable to our businesses than a new customer. And there is plenty of research to back it up: new customers are undoubtedly more expensive (most sources say five times more) to find and to attract than existing customers are to retain. At least that ought to be the case if we are looking after our customers properly. If we are, as we should be, delivering on our promises and fulfilling needs and wants to create truly satisfied, truly loyal customers. The genuinely loyal customer has a number of benefits to the business. They tend to be less demanding/difficult (and thus less draining of resource). They are less price sensitive than non-loyal customers. They buy more, and more often. And they can become ambassadors or customer-advocates for the brand.

There is a great deal of talk in marketing about 'customer loyalty'. The oft-described ideal is to take the customer along what might be called the 'line of loyalty': from new customer, to satisfied customer, to regular customer, to loyal customer, to customer-advocate. The last describes the dream customer who is voluntarily and enthusiastically championing your product, service and brand to everyone they meet.

But there are bear pits to watch out for on this apparently desirable path. The most obvious of course is at the 'new' customer stage. Your company will quite possibly have spent massive resources to get a potential customer to the point of purchase: but even when the purchase has taken place you cannot assume success, because something in the experience may have dissatisfied the customer: and as is well known, they may not tell you about it. They may simply never buy from you again, or worse, they may well tell others (many others if they are active on Twitter or TripAdvisor for example) about their dissatisfaction.

Even if they are 'satisfied' with the purchase in every way, and become 'regular' customers the marketer cannot rest on her laurels. Satisfied customers are potentially dangerous creatures. They rarely complain and as such they are easy to take for granted: and as such they are highly vulnerable to being wooed by competitor activity. And of course being a 'regular' customer is not as such an indication of any kind of commitment or connection: regularity may simply be a function of geographical convenience (as with most supermarket shoppers for example), or price.

Taking the customer to the point of genuine 'loyalty' is one of the most difficult steps in the whole marketing process: because loyalty is concerned with and dependent upon emotional engagement. Customer loyalty has two key elements:

1. The customer's rational understanding that they are receiving value (encompassing product and service quality, combined with what they perceive as appropriate pricing);
2. The customer's emotional engagement with the brand (which is dependent on a variety of elements that constitute a set of positive 'meanings').

This is quite a different definition of loyalty from that implied by loyalty cards and other such schemes (prevalent everywhere from coffee shops to airlines, from supermarkets, to high street retail chains, to dry cleaners). Loyalty cards would be more accurately described as 'regularity cards' in that, whilst they do appear to encourage regular purchase from the given store or brand, this is on the rational basis of receiving reward (points or discounts), rather than any emotional engagement.

So loyalty cards can appear to bring customers back on a regular basis, but that is not quite the same as real loyalty, which is important to note, because it does not therefore result in itself in helping customers towards the next step in the path: that of becoming 'customer advocates'. We shall come back to loyal customers and customer advocates later on.

THE MARKET AND THE INDUSTRY

A final few words in this chapter about the terms 'market' and 'marketing'. Of course the word market originally referred to the physical place where trading (exchange) actually took place. For our purposes though, and thus throughout this book, the word 'market' refers to the collection of people who buy (*actual* market) or might buy (*potential* market) your products or services.

You on the other hand (as the maker of product and the creator of services) are the 'industry'. In the modern era we are less inclined to barter like our cave dweller friends, and more likely to use money in one form or another as the method of exchange. Thus the simplest marketing model of all is simply described like this: the 'industry' provides products or services to the 'market' in exchange for money. In parallel with that exchange, in order to help it happen, the 'industry' communicates to the 'market' (telling it all about the products and services) and the 'market' provides information to the 'industry' (about its size, demography, needs, wants and demands).

Recent thinkers and practitioners often say that this simple circular system no longer adequately describes the reality. In the twenty-first century it seems that the communication (previously a one-way flow from 'industry' to 'market') is now a two-way conversation. And information (formerly a one-way flow in the other direction, from 'market; to 'industry') is now also two-way, with 'industry' and 'market' collaborating in product design, value propositions and so on.

WHO SAID IT . . .

"It's really hard to design products by focus groups. A lot of times, people don't know what they want until you show it to them."
– Steve Jobs

In many ways the boundaries between market and industry are becoming blurred. Many brands are now engaging customers in genuine conversations, allowing and encouraging customers to influence product and service design to an extent that goes far beyond traditional market research. More and more companies are creating online communities which not only stimulate discussion about the brand in question, but which also allow the brand to get under the skin of its customers and in turn give the customers a sense of 'ownership', which in turn can generate loyalty and advocacy.

But like all open conversations, this development carries the risk of misunderstanding and of causing offence. In 2010 the clothes retailer Gap notoriously asked its customers to submit designs for a new logo, having launched its own new design to widespread and severe criticism. Seeking input from the 'crowd' of customers in this way has become known as crowd-sourcing, but Gap got the crowd-sourcing approach wrong for two reasons. First because they asked their customers only after having launched their 'official' new logo and having realised that it was being met everywhere with mockery and scorn. So the resulting perception was that for Gap the customers were an afterthought, only consulted because of the negative reaction to the first logo. That was interpreted as a lack of respect for customers on the part of the brand. Second, because asking customers to provide a logo design was widely interpreted as 'cheap' and was attacked as unethical by wide sections of the design community, particularly in the United States.

It is no longer enough to think of a simple circular relationship between industry and market, and many marketers are embracing the notion of a more complex relationship with customers. Yet as the Gap example shows, it is very easy to misunderstand and mishandle the nuances and mores of this new style of relationship.

WHAT YOU NEED TO READ

▶ Philip Kotler's output is so vast and so extensively commented upon that perhaps the best place to begin investigating his thinking is on his website and in particular his answers to frequently asked questions www.kotlermarketing.com/phil_questions.shtml.

▶ Of Kotler's many books this is perhaps the best introductory example: *Kotler on Marketing*, Philip Kotler, Free Press, 2001.

▶ The hugely popular Seth Godin presents an excitingly irreverent take on marketing which balances Kotler's more academic stance. For an introduction to Godin see his daily blog www.sethgodin.typepad.com.

▶ For those who get the Godin bug this book demonstrates his style applied specifically to developing customer relationships: *Permission Marketing: turning strangers into friends and friends into customers*, Seth Godin, Pocket Books, 2007.

▶ Not strictly or exclusively marketing based, but always featuring the latest thinking and behaviour by many of the world's most dynamic and marketing-savvy entrepreneurs and businesses: www.fastcompany.com.

▶ For a thrilling account of the world's most famous marketing-oriented modern business-man see: *ICon, Steve Jobs: the greatest second act in the history of business,* J Young & W Simon, John Wiley & Sons Ltd, 2005.

IF YOU ONLY REMEMBER ONE THING

Marketing is not about selling the things you've made, but about making the things that people need and want.

CHAPTER 2

THE PRODUCT

WHAT IT'S ALL ABOUT

- ▶ Why products and services are at the heart of marketing
- ▶ The difference between products and services
- ▶ How consumer products differ from business-to-business products
- ▶ Why companies have to develop new products
- ▶ Why products have a life cycle
- ▶ Managing the product portfolio

At the very heart of marketing is the concept of 'product'. The product is what you take to market: the thing you have grown, raised, crafted, manufactured or developed in order to meet the needs and wants of your potential customers. But products come in many shapes and sizes, and often have no size or shape at all.

THE PRODUCT–SERVICE SPECTRUM

Products can be tangible or intangible. If they're tangible you can (by definition) touch them, and probably relate to them through other senses. Perfume and shampoo smell of something. Cooking sauces taste of something. Bicycles can be ridden. CDs and digital music downloads can be listened to, and newspapers read. Ovens can be turned on and off. T-shirts can be worn. And these tangible products have something else in common, in fact their most important common aspect: they can be kept and stored (on a shelf, in your fridge, your shed, your driveway, your wardrobe, or on your MP3 player).

You can't drop a digital music track on your foot, but it's still a product. Contrast that with a visit to a pub, a museum, or a hairdresser. Now whilst it's true that the visit to the pub involves products such as beer and nuts which you could theoretically take home (or indeed drop on your foot), and that a museum visit usually ends by exiting through the gift shop, it is also true that the visit itself – the service, or the experience if you like – cannot be stored (except in the memory).

So in these examples we have storable products on the one hand and non-storable services on the other. Reality though generally doesn't like such black and white, on or off distinctions. A more accurate picture would be a spectrum: a line with pure products at one end and pure service at the other. And why is it a spectrum? Why is it so hard to say 'that's a product' and 'that's a service'? Because if you think about the purchase of pure hard-edged (drop it on your foot) products such as a new television, it is terribly difficult to separate the product element in that purchase from the service you received. Which is why (notwithstanding their promise to be 'never knowingly undersold') shoppers loyal to John Lewis choose that store because of the service they receive as much as for the quality and price of the products available. So you are in John Lewis buying a fridge for example, but what are you actually paying for? The fridge alone? Or the fridge plus the service? Or the fridge, plus the service, plus the comforting notion that John Lewis will never knowingly break the trust which you have placed in it?

WHO SAID IT . . .

"There are no such things as service industries. There are only industries whose service components are greater or less than those of other industries. Everybody is in service."
– Theodore Levitt

Many offerings in the market are therefore somewhere along the notional product-service spectrum, rather than firmly at one end or the other. Some are products with a service element to some degree, whilst others are services with a product element. The hairdresser appears to be all service at first glance (you can't store your hair-style after all, at least not for long), but there is a product element, from the nice (or nasty) coffee that they serve you (or not) to the quality and pleasantness of the shampoos, conditioners, colours or with whatever else they anoint you, and which they hope you will purchase supplies of to take home.

Product service spectrum

| Pure product | Most products and services are on a spectrum | Pure service |

John Lewis is a classic example of a brand which enhances its product offering with a strong service offering in order to create differentiation. It's one of the reasons why John Lewis is such a consistently strong brand. But it's not always an easy path to walk, and the inclination towards service can come under acute pressure when there is strong price competition. In fact sometimes an entire sector can become so price-led, so commoditised, that it reaches a point where adding service is seen by the market (the customers) as adding cost rather than adding value.

There is then a real intellectual and emotional battle for the committed marketer to fight. Do they follow the drive to the bottom of the possible market, cutting prices and creating ever cheaper products or services, or do they differentiate themselves from the melee by committing to a strong service element?

Think of the (highly commoditised) insurance sector. Vast amounts of advertising are created to promote comparison websites where we can measure and compare the features we get from different insurance products, and their prices, against their competitors. Sectors don't come much more commoditised than that, and yet there are some notable exceptions: insurance providers who make an overt virtue of not appearing on comparison sites. Instead what they ask you to do is to trust them to provide the best product (and price) combined with a 'service' aspect which (they imply) you won't receive from the price-led offerings on the comparison sites.

EXPERIENCES

As if the blurring between products and services wasn't fuzzy enough, brands in many sectors are increasingly focused on creating a third category of offering: known as 'customer experiences'.

Experiences in this sense are neither tangible (drop, foot, ouch) nor intangible (polite staff, quick delivery, pleasant shopping environment), but rather something that doesn't quite fit on the simple product–service spectrum. Experiences refers to our memories of what happened and how we felt when we bought the 'thing' and interacted with it. Experiences aren't stored in the cupboard, or on the iPad: they are stored inside our heads and hearts. They are 'internalised'. You might argue that we can indeed store our memories as pictures or video. But they aren't really the memories themselves, rather they are reminders of the memories.

Look at any holiday brochure, or at the literature or advertising promoting almost any car brand, or the marketing materials of the business class tickets of long-haul airlines, and you will see how the notion of experiences has taken hold. Hotels and airlines used to make service promises, but now they promise 'experiences'. Car manufacturers used to make performance, comfort and status promises, but now they promise 'experiences'. BMW, for example, has lately been offering 'Joy'. Clearly a BMW, like any car, is a product (it is self-evidently tangible and storable): but what the manufacturer teases us with is not the product itself, but an experience.

We buy an airline ticket because we want the service of travelling from point A to point B, but we are inclined, if we have the resources, to buy a business class or first-class ticket, not simply to alleviate the perceived discomfort of travelling economy, but because we want a particular experience.

And experiences are most self-evident in the world of leisure and entertainment. From a visit to Disneyworld to spending several hours playing the latest Playstation game, what is being purchased might at first glance look like a product (video game) or a service (rides and other entertainments courtesy of Disney), but what is actually valued by the customer in these cases is the 'experience'. Perhaps the zenith (literally and figuratively) of the consumable experience is Richard Branson's Virgin Galaxy enterprise, with tickets for short rides in the stratosphere priced at around £400000. Such is the desirability of this experience that Branson has sold a lot of tickets, though the craft itself has yet to be built.

THREE LEVELS OF A PRODUCT

In their book *Marketing*, Baines, Fill and Page explain products slightly differently, as a kind of Aztec pyramid of three levels which they call Core, Embodied and Augmented.

At the top of the pyramid is the Core Product. This represents the real, core, essential 'benefit' to you as the customer. It can be a functional benefit (you can now drive your car to your meeting) or it can be emotional (relief, ceasing of anxiety, ability to focus on the meeting), or both.

On the middle level is the Embodied Product which describes the actual physical goods or the actual service received. This embodiment includes a wide range of factors, from the product features, its durability, effectiveness, user-friendliness of design, packaging, even the brand name and its associations.

On the base level, supporting the other two levels, is the Augmented Product which refers to all the other elements which enable the Embodied Product to be delivered to the market. The Augmented Product covers elements as diverse as credit, training, delivery times, guarantees, and customer perceptions of service.

The curious but rather profound thing about this model is that at first sight it is easy to think it's the wrong way up. But it isn't. Because way before we, as marketers, get to deliver a 'benefit' to our customers (the Core Product) we have to address the other building blocks first. Not to do so is to live in a fantasy world where customer benefit (and therefore profitable business) can simply be conjured up out of the air. Get these building blocks the wrong way round and we'll be busy making marvellous promises to our customers which we'll singularly fail to keep.

Three levels of product

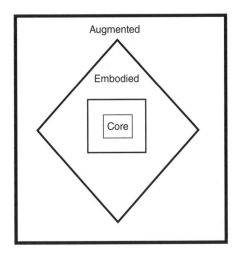

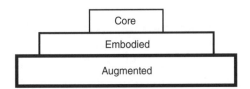

CLASSIFYING 'CONSUMER' PRODUCTS

A key step in analysing a company's marketing efficacy is to analyse its products, and that analysis begins with classifying them. It's important simply because 'product' can mean a number of different things. First we'll look at 'consumer' products. Later we'll look at 'business' products.

A well-established, perhaps the classic, classification of products is to decide whether they are 'durable' or 'non-durable'. Durables are things that are going to last for some (indeterminate but lengthy) period of time, such as bicycles, fridges (and other so-called white goods), cameras, cars. Non-durables are, as you'd expect, those products which have a much shorter lifespan. Yoghurt for example (because it will soon be mouldy), or ball-point pens because they will run out of ink.

And then, as we've discussed, there are services.

DEGREES OF CONSUMER INVOLVEMENT

Durables and non-durables differ not only in their lifespan, but in what is called 'consumer involvement'. The theory goes that durable goods demand and excite a higher level of involvement from consumers, who will do more research into their possible purchase options, and take more time over the purchase, because by definition their commitment to the product is going to be longer. You'll have your fridge in your kitchen longer than you'll have your yoghurt in the fridge. The financial investment is higher too, and therefore the risk is higher. Choose a car of a particular colour which you didn't really like (because it was cheaper) and you're most likely going to be wincing when you get into it for the next several years.

Non-durables, it follows, are less involving. They are lower risk, lower cost, and lower commitment. Nevertheless, we live in ever-changing times, and it is clear that often there is substantial involvement (intellectual, emotional, ethical and even moral) in the purchase of non-durable goods. Some people will only buy organic food produce for example. Others will only buy fair-trade. Others will only invest in ethical financial products. And so on. So the fairly simple durable v. non-durable classification isn't quite sufficient on its own.

There is a more profound way to classify a company's consumer products, and that is according to the behaviour that consumers actually adopt when they are buying. It looks at products through the consumers' eyes, if you will.

In this model there are once again three product types.

CONVENIENCE PRODUCTS

These are typically products which don't prompt the buyer to put in much thought, emotion or effort. They are usually relatively inexpensive, and they are bought relatively frequently. An important characteristic of convenience products is that, as you would expect from something which doesn't command much emotional commitment, they also fail to command brand loyalty. If we can't find our habitual brand of convenience product, we are unlikely to leave the shop to start a search: instead we will choose an alternative brand, or the shop's 'own label' product. Convenience products can be further divided into three sub-types:

1. *Staple* products: the stuff of daily life, from foods like bread and milk, to petrol, to newspapers, and (if you're so inclined) cigarettes.
2. *Impulse* products: things you haven't set out to buy or planned for but which grab your attention in the moment, from bars of chocolate, to flowers, to a magazine, to small gift items for an irritable child.
3. *Emergency* products: things you buy when a particular, often unforeseen, need arises. Lightbulbs, plasters, umbrellas all fall into this category, as would a particular food item that you suddenly discover you need, such as ketchup, stuffing mix, butter.

An overall characteristic of convenience products is that they are relatively easily substituted.

SHOPPING PRODUCTS

So-called 'shopping' products aren't bought as frequently as convenience products, so they do involve some degree of 'research' by the consumer, or sometimes just a bit of familiarisation with what's available: it's the active 'shopping around' element which gives these products their name. In other words the consumer has a tendency to look in several stores, or to look at different options online, or to ask friends for their opinions, or to read reviews, before buying. Mobile phones are classic 'shopping' products. As are electrical goods with limited lifespan, such as irons. Some furniture and equally some insurance products also fit into this category.

Brand loyalty might be very low in this category (when our iron breaks down we may just compare a few different irons for features/benefits/price in our favourite department store regardless of brand). On the other hand brand can play a big role here and it's a powerful place for brands to operate. Mobile phones, despite the huge commodity-like emphasis on tariffs and contracts, is also highly influenced by brand. You will notice, if you threaten to leave one provider at the end of your contract, that special 'retention' offers will appear out of nowhere to tempt you to another contract.

There are usually substitutes available for shopping products, but there is a greater tendency from the consumer to keep searching until they find the thing they feel offers the greatest benefit (actual or perceived).

SPECIALITY PRODUCTS

Speciality products involve more 'risk' and thus more commitment and more attention from the consumer. Speciality products may be bought only very infrequently or even once in a lifetime. They are usually relatively expensive. A cruise trip. A celebratory dinner for the extended family and friends at a swanky restaurant. A prestige car. An original painting. A high-end set of golf clubs. The top of the range guitar that's long been coveted. An expensive watch. A haute couture ball-gown. A yacht!

Not only does this category command the most research and effort from the consumer, but it also involves the highest degree of emotional, as well as intellectual involvement. In the end, and somewhat counter-intuitively, evidence indicates that despite extensive research by the consumer, he or she will ultimately make their purchase with their heart and not their head. The choice between a Rolex, an Omega and a Patek Philippe may involve considerable 'research' in the sense of looking at and handling many different watches, but the decision will be an emotional one (but one which many consumers will rationalise after the fact).

Speciality products often have very few substitutes, or no substitutes at all. One successful client of mine, for example, will only ever write with Mont Blanc pens and drive Maseratis. There were, for her, both literally and figuratively, no substitutes. For the less brand-committed there may some substitutes but they will be small in number: there aren't that many different high end cruise fleets or that many makers of professional standard gold clubs.

For each of these categories, because the customers' attitude and behaviour is different, the marketing strategy also has to differ.

WHO YOU NEED TO KNOW
Howard Schultz

Not actually the original founder of Starbucks, but the real creator of the brand as it is known around the world today. Schultz's great marketing insight was two-fold. First, that people all over the USA and ultimately the world could be persuaded to pay a premium for a distinctive high-quality product, which raised coffee above its mundane commodity beverage status. Second, that people would pay an even greater premium for the 'experience' of drinking their new and better coffee in a relaxed and comfortable environment, which Starbucks referred to as *the third* place (neither home nor work). Schultz's aggressive expansion of the chain has been much criticised, and it could be argued that the original promise which made the brand so distinct has been weakened by over-stretching. Nevertheless the Starbucks vision is something of a masterclass in the imaginative marriage of product and experience.

WE'RE ALL IN THE SERVICE BUSINESS

Unlike the drop on your foot characteristics of products, services are less tangible, but of course no less powerful or real. Services, to qualify for the name, really have to give some benefit to the customer, but that benefit can be emotional, sensory, intellectual or even spiritual as much as 'actual'. Services are generally time and place dependent, in other words they happen somewhere at a particular time and you can't take them away and put them somewhere to store. And of course, unlike a product, you don't end up by 'owning' the service: it doesn't become yours.

Theodore Levitt says we are all in the service business, but I think he would acknowledge that in a 'service' (more than with a 'product') the service provider himself or herself is a very real part of the service received. In other words a massage in an airport lounge spa is very nice, but it would be much less so if delivered by an aggressive and rough practitioner.

Although services can be complex and multi-faceted in their benefits to the customer, a service will generally have one essential or core benefit. A nice haircut makes you look better. Having your car serviced makes it work more reliably. Your dentist will take your toothache away. And if the core benefit is not delivered for some reason, then peripheral benefits will not have much value. A disastrous haircut will not be compensated by nice coffee.

Oddly enough though, continuing with the example of the hairdresser, it is perfectly possible to deliver a consistently excellent core benefit (good haircut) but to fail or be inconsistent in the peripherals (coffee and conversation say) and to lose customers that way. Michael Gerber in his book *The E-Myth Revisited* tells a story precisely of that nature about his experience with a barber, who whilst excellent at haircuts was inconsistent (not bad, note, just inconsistent) in the provision of other experiential benefits, and thus quickly lost Gerber's trust and eventually his custom.

We've already seen how services cannot be stored or transported like products. You have to go the theatre to see the play (or rather to see it in the uniquely atmospheric environment of the theatre). You have to be in the hotel in order to sleep in the room. But that's not to say that all services are fixed in this way. You no longer have to be in the bank to do your banking after all.

It is often said that one notable characteristic of services is that they are, by virtue of being provided by humans, inconsistent in nature. That is clearly true to a degree, but not absolutely. The training of McDonald's staff, and the detailed structure of the brand's service procedures, is such that your experience of McDonald's service will be remarkably consistent wherever you go in your country (and even across the world, subject to language and some cultural differences). The consistency of human service from First Direct staff is the key reason that people remain loyal to that brand for so long.

There is another aspect to inconsistency in service too, which is that it is not always or necessarily a negative. In Pret A Manger sandwich shops baristas are empowered to offer free coffee at their discretion to regular customers. It is inconsistent in that you can't rely on receiving a free coffee, but its inconsistency is part of its charm. The clever trick that Pret pull off here is being positively inconsistent with an otherwise highly consistent (and high quality) offering. And of course being over-consistent can easily become inflexibility, which is ultimately dehumanising and alienating (which is why First Direct's commitment to having humans answer the phone stands out so sharply from most other banks and their 'choose option 1' approach).

BUSINESS PRODUCTS

By definition business products, which are bought by businesses to satisfy a 'rational' need, should tend to be selected and purchased in a more rational way than is the case for consumer products. But that isn't always the case of course. Business buyers are people first, and as such are hugely influenced by emotion, including the emotions triggered by brand and by perceived or actual customer experience.

Remember the old saying 'no-one ever got fired for choosing IBM'? A classic example of how an apparently rational, researched, purchasing decision can be influenced by prejudice, anxiety, loyalty or any number of other emotions.

Nevertheless, with that caveat in mind, let's look briefly at the six main categories of business products:

1. **Equipment**

   Bought by businesses in two further sub-categories:

   ▶ Capital Equipment: including buildings purchased, heavy plant, factory machinery, roads, even hospitals and other similar large scale investments. They tend to cost a lot of money and to be long-term projects with a complicated multi-level purchasing process.

   ▶ Accessory equipment: much simpler stuff like photocopiers, furniture, computers and so on. Price, brand, service and sales relationship all play a role in the marketing process here.

2. **Materials**

   Including commodities like chemicals, minerals, food, paper. The purchase process centres around price but there is a strong element of relationship-building and trust at the sales-customer interface.

3. **Semi-finished goods**

   One step further along the value chain from raw materials, semi-finished goods include sheets of steel, bolts of cloth, rolls of printing paper.

4. **MRO goods (maintenance, repair and operating)**
   Literally the nuts and bolts of business, including light bulbs, pens and pencils, USB sticks, CD-ROMs, machine oil, cleaning fluids, repair tools, and nuts and bolts.

5. **Components**
   Items purchased as finished from one company and used by another to complete its own product, such as a car maker buying complete headlamp assemblies or seat-belt fittings, or a bicycle manufacturer buying gear sets and saddles.

6. **Services**
   From public relations to IT support, accountancy to contract cleaning.

THE LIFE-CYCLE OF PRODUCTS

Products, though inanimate, are far from static, though some manufacturers make the mistake of assuming that their product, once created, has a permanent and unchanging value in the eye of the customer (business or consumer). The reality though is that the market constantly shifts and therefore any given product also shifts in relation to it. A product, let's say a daily newspaper in 1970, had a particular value in the market on the day of its publication. Even a day later, of course, its value is massively diminished. But the really important shift in value is not really to do with old news, but to do with the bigger change in the market between 1970 and now. In 40 years the value of the daily newspaper in its traditional form has declined enormously. The product is the same in general, but the market has moved on.

WHO SAID IT . . .

"A market is never saturated with a good product, but it is very quickly saturated with a bad one."
– Henry Ford

The picture is made more complex still because of the specific life-cycle of a given product, even aside from the shift in the market place. It is, you might say, a highly dynamic system.

The classic description of the life-cycle, which can apply to individual products, or brands, or even entire categories, covers five stages: Development, Introduction, Growth, Maturity, and Decline.

As the following Product life cycle diagram shows, sales have a tendency to increase to a high-point when the product is considered 'mature' and then to decline. Profits meanwhile follow a similar arc, with the difference that during the development and introduction stage the profits are actually losses.

Product life cycle

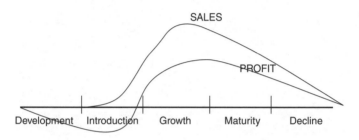

It's a pretty good description of what happens, and it would be extremely useful for the marketer and the company in general, but for one glaring problem: it's virtually impossible to know exactly where you are in the life-cycle. Well that's not strictly true. You know when you're in Development because you're spending money like water and everyone is panicking about getting your product finished and ready for market. And you know when you're in Introduction because you've spent a fortune launching your product and you've sold at least some of them! But from then on in it's pretty much a guessing game, because your Introduction stage might last weeks, months or years, and you'll only know it's over when it's over.

Even when Maturity becomes Decline you still don't know for sure what the timescales will be. The daily newspaper has been in steady decline for decades, but we can still buy papers every day. I know a real-ale brewing company which has grown steadily and strongly despite the decline of the real-ale market over more than two decades. A few years ago the market for small independent bookshops looked to be completely over. Now the market is growing again. Just a few decades ago cinemas were closing. Now movie attendances are higher than ever. Nothing in marketing can be taken for granted.

NEW PRODUCT DEVELOPMENT

It's a widely expressed but little understood truth that new products usually fail. It's hard to quote any meaningful statistics for that because there are so many variables and so many sources of information. Suffice to say here that many more products go through Development than actually get to enjoy Growth, Maturity and Decline. Many more of course don't even get to Introduction and are pulled because of excessive costs, poor performance in research, getting beaten to the starting line by competitors, or good old-fashioned cold-feet.

Peter Drucker says there are three key reasons for new product failure. They are simple and yet profound, and they also make clear why so many enthusiastic but naive entrepreneurs fail to succeed.

1. There is no market for it (nobody wants to buy your widget).
2. There is a market need but the product doesn't meet it (people would buy your widget if only it were smaller, lighter, faster, cheaper, more stylish, etc.).
3. There is a market need and the product meets the need but you have failed to communicate (your widget is great, but your advertising or PR or other marketing-communications aren't working).

THE NEW PRODUCT IMPERATIVE

Introducing new products is expensive, time-consuming and hugely risky, and yet it cannot be avoided. New products are not only absolutely key to gaining competitive advantage, but arguably they are fundamental to the existence (certainly to the continued existence) of any business. If you make products or provide services then generally speaking there is a market imperative for you to continuously develop and launch new products and services. Imagine Apple without new product development. Inconceivable of course.

WHO SAID IT . . .

"Life is pretty simple: You do some stuff. Most fails. Some works. You do more of what works. If it works big, others quickly copy it. Then you do something else. The trick is the doing something else."
– Tom Peters

New products, for all their challenges, offer a range of benefits, as follows:

1. A new product can increase or protect your market share by giving your potential customer more opportunities to choose you rather than your competitors.
2. A new product can give you something to sell to a different segment of your market (my example real-ale brewer Adnams has just announced plans to distil high quality English whisky).
3. New products enhance your reputation for innovation (as Apple proves every few weeks).
4. New products can spread your risk by diversifying into different markets or niches, although of course in a sense you have created new risk.

5. New products can help you make fuller and more effective use of your production capacity (the classic, if quirky, example being Procter & Gamble originally making Pringles using the same production process as their soap products).

6. New products can level out your demand across the year or other time period (which is why universities are so active in the conference business, and why greetings card manufacturers love to create and popularise new holidays).

WHO YOU NEED TO KNOW
Martin Lindstrom

Listed by *Time* magazine in 2009 as one of the world's most influential people, Lindstrom is a brand expert with a difference: his work is primarily concerned with the scientifically observable effect on consumers of their experiences of brands, advertising and actual products. The subtitle of his bestseller

Buyology: How everything we believe about why we buy is wrong gives a strong hint of his iconoclastic and populist but ruthlessly analytical approach to marketing. Lindstrom, one of the most distinctive and colourful characters in marketing, is an advisor for numerous global clients including McDonald's, Disney, Microsoft and Unilever and the author of several other bestselling books including *Brand Sense* which examines the influence of our senses on our buying behaviour.

NOT EVERY NEW PRODUCT IS REALLY NEW

New products come in many shapes and colours, so to speak. Some new products are genuinely new inventions (from the motor car to the MP3 player, from the Dyson cleaner to the electric guitar). But the term 'new product' can equally be applied to engineering variants or developments of existing products, or new colours or flavours, even the re-packaging and re-naming of old products for a different market niche. There are five main types:

1. *Innovative* products which genuinely make a breakthrough, often technological, though not exclusively.
2. *Replacement* products which give us the latest version of something with which we are already familiar. The VW Golf is in its sixth iteration now I think.
3. *Variant* products, which offer a different spin on the established product, from a new flavour of pizza to a 'World Cup' edition football.
4. *Me-too* products which lean heavily on the innovation carried out by someone else and are literally saying to the market 'we've got one of those too'. A trip to the supermarket will demonstrate hundreds of me-too products of every kind.
5. *Relaunched* products which are really old products refined, redeveloped, and re-presented to the market. Some will look completely new (because you didn't notice them first time round). Others will be knowingly 'retro' reinventions of something for which we might have a nostalgic fondness, and others just a last-ditch attempt to save a declining product from extinction.

MANAGING THE PRODUCT PORTFOLIO

Most businesses will have more than one product or service in the market at any one time, and the degree of attention and resource to direct at any particular product in the portfolio is a constant worry to marketers. One of the best known models in the whole marketing literature addresses this problem. Devised by the Boston Consulting Group it has become known simply as the Boston matrix.

Boston matrix

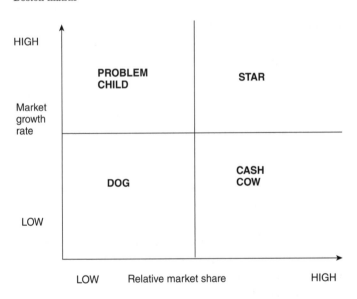

The Boston Matrix gives marketers a handy tool for assessing products within the company's portfolio. Two measures are applied to a product: does it have a relatively high or low share of its market, and is that market growing?

Star products or brands in the portfolio enjoy a winning combination of a large share of a growing market. It's a great place to be but it requires investment, innovation and careful management to stay ahead.

Cash Cows have a high share of their market too, but the market is growing more slowly, or may be static, or even in decline. The product may be immensely valuable nevertheless and can be 'milked' for cash whilst still profitable. Cash Cows can often fund the investment required by Stars, but they must not be neglected or starved or they will turn into Dogs.

Dogs are products with a relatively small share of a slow-growing, static or declining market. The general advice given about product Dogs is to 'shoot 'em', but they can frequently be sold off. Dogs do need to be dealt with though, or they will drain resources which would be much better utilised elsewhere.

Problem Child products are those which have a relatively small share of a growing market, and therein lies the problem. If the market continues to grow then they can be profitable, but to really grow share requires resource and cash investment. Playing safe is actually dangerous too though: because just being in a market at all costs money, and if the opportunity is not being maximised it might be better to sell off the Problem Child. Yet, a Problem Child, given the right investment, can become a star. The marketer's classic dilemma.

SUPPLY AND DEMAND OF PRODUCTS

There was a time when the job of marketing was relatively simple. If you offered a decent product which people wanted, and if you did so at a competitive price, and were of a pleasant enough demeanour and therefore gave acceptable service, then you stood a pretty good chance of selling your products and making a living.

But this simplicity was shattered swiftly by the advent of mass production, transport infrastructure, urbanisation of the population and the physical separation of producer and customer (which is to say that the furniture-maker was no longer visited in his workshop by the prospective buyer, and the farmer no longer personally brought her goods to sell in the market). All of these changes led to increased competition and to the need for active marketing.

In the introduction to this book I give a simple example of exchange (sharpened flint for freshly caught meat) but we are long since past the simplicity of this system. Now we still exchange, but we exchange money (in one form or another), and you have to remember that when we do so we are not exchanging things (or things in return for money) of equal value.

That sounds counter-intuitive, but it is a vital concept at the centre of what marketing is about. No, we aren't exchanging 'equal' value: each party in the trade is exchanging something of 'lower value to them' for something of 'higher value to them'. How can this be? Because value is always relative and 'perceived'. You might be a skilled DIY practitioner, perfectly capable of fitting a new kitchen for example. The question though is whether you value the time you would have to sacrifice to do that job more highly or not than the money which you will have to pay a kitchen fitter to do the job for you.

FROM SUPPLY-LED TO DEMAND-DRIVEN

Which brings us to supply and demand in the market. There are two kinds of market. In a supply-led market the challenge is to produce enough to meet customer need: to keep up with demand! You might say that doesn't happen too often, but it's exactly what happened when Apple launched their iPad device, to the extent that they had to postpone the UK launch to allow them to produce enough units.

In a demand-driven market the challenge is different: to meet customer wants whilst fighting off competitors trying to do the same.

That might sound all rather theoretical, but understanding it makes a huge difference to a company's chances of success or failure.

In the supply-led scenario you have to decide whether to produce as many widgets as you can in order to maximise sales and profits by satisfying every possible customer, or to play it a bit safe, under-produce and therefore not satisfy every customer or exploit every sales opportunity (but at least not have heaps of unwanted widgets left over).

In the demand-driven scenario you might want to think twice about making enough widgets for everyone, because you're likely to end up with the heaps of unsold widgets and thus lower margins and lower profits.

There is a theoretical point where all goods are sold and all potential customers satisfied, and the optimum price achieved. Theoretical, and of course unachievable. But a key objective of marketing is to get as close to that point as possible: matching production (or the provision of services or creation of experiences) as closely as possible to the needs and wants of the customers, and at a price and in a manner which will encourage them to buy as much as possible of what you are offering. And all the time the marketer must take care that their offering is neither too cheap (because their profit margin will be diminished, and they may therefore either fail to meet demand or indeed scare off their customers because of perceived lack of quality) nor too expensive (because they may attract fewer customers and fail to sell their product in sufficient numbers to make a healthy profit).

Marketing is ultimately a balancing act between supply and demand.

WHAT YOU NEED TO READ

▶ Steve Jobs' legendary keynote presentations to the Apple faithful never fail to demonstrate why Apple's constant product innovation is crucial in the company's success: www.apple.com/apple-events/september-2010.

▶ An accessible and clear introduction into how businesses successfully (or otherwise) cope with new product development: *Innovation Management and New Product Development*, Dr Paul Trott, Financial Times/Prentice Hall, 2008 (4th edn).

▶ Computer scientist Donald Norman is widely regarded as one of the world's greatest contemporary thinkers on design, and particularly on humans' relationships with the products around them. His book *Emotional Design: why we love (or hate) everyday things*, Basic Books, 2003, is a salutary lesson for those who think consumers are blind to the difference between good and bad products.

▶ Honing right in on the customer experience challenge and how to create positive experiences is *Build Great Customer Experiences*, Colin Shaw & John Ivens, Palgrave Macmillan, 2002.

▶ Over the past three decades company after company has made a strategic shift from making products to providing services. This book looks deep into the lessons from the successful and less successful transitions: *From Products to Services: Insights and experience from companies which have embraced the service economy*, Laurie Young, John Wiley & Sons Ltd, 2008.

▶ For a first-person account of a real product developer cum marketer's journey James Dyson's autobiography *Against The Odds*, Texere, 2000, turns the unpromising topic of the vacuum cleaner industry into a powerful guide to creating successful products within a mature market.

IF YOU ONLY REMEMBER ONE THING

The experiences that companies give to customers are just as important in creating customer value as the products and services being purchased.

CHAPTER 3
THE MARKET

WHAT IT'S ALL ABOUT

- ▶ Understanding the marketing environment
- ▶ Dividing the market into manageable chunks
- ▶ Choosing a target audience
- ▶ Taking a 'position'
- ▶ The attitude and behaviour of the buyer

Businesses can never operate in a vacuum. They are intimately connected to their environment in a host of ways, and their success or failure is hugely influenced by what happens around them. A vital task of the marketer is to observe, analyse, understand and respond to this 'market environment'.

ENVIRONMENTAL SCANNING

Looking closely at the environment in which the business operates has two main benefits. First, it provides a firm foundation to the whole planning process. In other words, before the marketer can decide what to do and how and where to do it, they must appreciate the existing market situation. Second, by continuing to observe and analyse the marketer is not only able to make judgements about their company's activity (and to alter it accordingly), but also to respond productively to opportunities and threats presented by changes in the market or in the activity of competitors.

The process of 'scanning' the environment is (as the term implies) never really finished, but should be ongoing: a permanent lookout watching the environment. It has been described as having five stages:

1. Monitoring of trends, issues and events.
2. Identifying which of the observed events are of significance.

3. Evaluating the likely (and even unlikely) effect of those events.
4. Making predictions about how things will develop.
5. Evaluating once again (all the time continuing to monitor).

One popular model for enabling this scanning is PEST, which looks at the environment under the four aspect headings: Political, Economic, Social and Technological. The model doesn't provide easy answers but can help to organise the marketer's thinking. The PEST model has been extended to include further categories, including Legal and Environmental issues (becoming PESTLE), but a more detailed and carefully structured approach was devised by Pickton and Broderick in their book *Integrated Marketing Communications.*

Their PRESTCOM model builds on PEST to look at 'external', the 'competitive' and the 'internal' influencing factors, shown in the following diagram, as three concentric circles of influence.

At the heart of the environment (the Internal) lies the organisation itself. Of course the 'Organisational' heading is just that, a heading, and the wise marketer

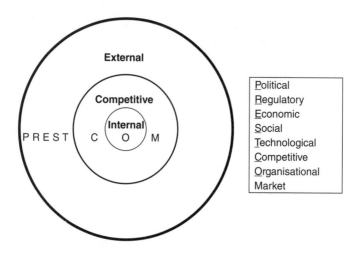

will look into the full gamut of internal/organisational elements, from human resources to R&D, and from finance to the priorities of the board.

WHO SAID IT . . .

"There is nothing like looking, if you want to find something. You certainly usually find something, if you look, but it is not always quite the something you were after."
– **J. R. R. Tolkien**

LOOKING AT THE COMPETITION

Surrounding the Internal environment is the Competitive environment, which looks at the Market itself (customers) and at the actual competitors to the business. Competition comes in many shapes and sizes, and is sometimes unrecognised as a threat. It is not at all uncommon to hear new entrepreneurs as well as senior people in large corporations claim to have 'no real competition'. Sadly such claims are almost always wrong. Competition can be divided broadly into four types:

1. Direct competitors are those businesses who offer products or services very similar to your own. Cadbury's Dairy Milk is direct competition to Galaxy for example. Virgin Atlantic is directly competitive with British Airways on certain routes, as is Barclays with NatWest.

2. Close competitors are just that. They may not be precisely similar (and there is therefore a danger of not viewing them as competition) but they overlap in some way. Budget airlines such as Ryanair are not providing exactly the same service as the 'full service' airlines, but they are nevertheless close competition and may be chosen for specific reasons even by flyers who would normally fly with more expensive providers. Pret A Manger is a sandwich store whereas Starbucks is a coffee shop, and they vary in both product and experience, but they are nevertheless close competitors.

3. Substitute competitors are different but manage to fulfill the need or want. Guinness is a 'substitute' competitor with virtually every real ale brand, because although quite different from anything in the real ale category, it has enough in common to be part of the beer drinker's repertoire (and research shows that real-ale drinkers will frequently select Guinness in the absence of their preferred tipple). A supermarket cook-at-home Chinese meal in a box is a substitute competitor not only with a local Chinese takeaway, but also with a local fish and chip shop. On certain journeys (say from London to Glasgow) train and plane are substitute competitors for each other.

4. Indirect competitors are those which may not have any great similarity in themselves, but which compete for share of time and wallet. 'Shall we go to the movies or for a pizza?'. 'Shall I buy this book or that DVD?'.

WHO YOU NEED TO KNOW
Peter Doyle

One of the great marketing theorists and a globally recognised teacher and researcher of marketing and business strategy. Peter Doyle, who died aged 59 in 2003 was the initiator of the concept of value-based marketing. Doyle's numerous papers on the topic, and his seminal book *Value-Based Marketing: marketing strategies for corporate growth and shareholder value* helped to place marketing at the boardroom table by making the strongest rational (and research-based) case for its contribution to a business as a whole. Philip Kotler himself described the book as 'a tipping point' in the maturing of marketing as a business force. Doyle was an academic, but a practical one, and his book provides a workable blueprint for undertaking marketing in a rational and results-oriented way.

THE THREAT FROM COMPETITORS

Businesses are threatened by competition in a variety of ways, famously defined as five forces by competitive strategy expert Michael Porter. According to Porter, as shown in the following diagram, any business in any marketplace is not only caught in a whirlwind of rivalry with existing competitors (whom at least have the virtue of being known 'enemies'), but is also under more or less constant threat of assault from four other forces which are perhaps less easy to spot and to tackle.

The rivalry between competitors is often manifested in highly competitive advertising and other promotional activity, the drive to innovate with new and improved products, and the jostling for 'position' in the minds and hearts of the market.

Meanwhile, outside of the battle with rivals, the first force at play is the threat of new entrants. There are almost always new entrants gathering on the borders of any market, hoping to steal market share. The threat of new entrants is directly related to the strength and height of what are known as 'barriers to entry'. If a market is costly and time consuming to enter because of technological investment required (say mobile technology devices or pharmaceuticals) or because of manufacturing challenges (making cars for example) then barriers to entry are said to be high and the threat from new entrants relatively low. But barriers can disappear with terrifying

Porter's five forces

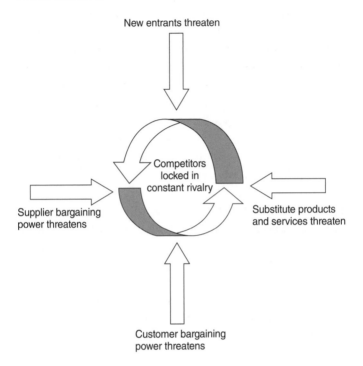

swiftness, falling virtually overnight through technological advances, legislative changes, falling costs of human and other resources, and other factors.

The second threatening force comes from substitutes who, whilst they are not actually trying to take market share, have the effect of putting restriction on prices and of limiting competitive advantage.

The third stems from the bargaining power of customers. In some circumstances this can have a powerful effect on profitability. We've all seen in the media stories of how large supermarket chains dictate tough terms to their suppliers (in this scenario the supermarket is the customer of course). And with the rise of the internet-driven comparison website the ability of customers to make direct price comparisons is a notable limiting factor upon the prices that insurance or utility companies can charge (unless, as sometimes seems to be the case, an entire industry moves as one).

The fourth external force lies in the bargaining power of the suppliers. Producers of relatively rare raw materials (crude oil for example) can sometimes dictate prices to their customers, as can some very powerful brands. Every single high street mobile phone retailer wants to stock the iPhone, which puts Apple in an enviably powerful bargaining position, in which they control both the wholesale and the retail price by forbidding discounting.

MARKET SEGMENTATION

It's a truism that people are different. And being different, people need and want different things. But it is also a truism that no company, no matter how ambitious or how well resourced, can possibly produce an infinite variety of products (or even an infinite range of variants of a single product).

In the relatively recent era of mass marketing (which lasted roughly three quarters of a century, from the advent of mass production in industry in the early 1900s through to the rise of internet towards the end of the millennium) large companies had a tendency to ignore the 'different' needs and wants of individuals and to concentrate instead on the mass of the population.

WHO SAID IT . . .

"Market segmentation is a natural result of the vast differences among people."
– **Donald Norman**

They were helped in this self-assured behaviour by virtue of operating in the supply-led era which mass production heralded. Success in that heady age stemmed from the production of affordable goods in high enough numbers to meet the huge demand of western society's rapidly growing demand for a new and improved lifestyle and all its component parts. At its height this era of mass marketing was represented most dramatically and seductively by advertising in its most glamorous and creative form, on TV, on billboards, in the cinema and in the press. Advertising by almost universally recognised brands which was seen, absorbed and frequently discussed by enormous proportions of the population. From Coca Cola to Ford, to Daz, to Silk Cut, to Cadbury's Smash, and so on, brands didn't have to worry about the individuality of their customers. The secret to marketing lay in attracting attention, exciting interest and desire, and keeping up with demand.

But that era is gone. Marketers now operate in a much more 'choosy' era which is demand-driven rather than supply-led, and in this new world it simply isn't effective any more (except arguably for a very few 'heritage' brands who have such a strong position in the market that they can still more or less get away with the old mass-market techniques). However, the death of the mass-market didn't happen overnight, and during that era's demise marketers were busy preparing for the new world.

Fundamental to the post mass-market outlook are the concepts of market segmentation and targeting.

Segmentation refers to the dividing up of a market into manageable and meaningful chunks, each of which consists of people (all markets are of course made of people) who have some similar characteristics. Of course it is impossible in reality for marketers to find segments which consist of people identical in every respect (no matter how desirable that might be from the company's point of view), so segmentation doesn't try to achieve that. Instead segmentation attempts to divide a market into groups of people who are similar enough to others within a given group, and different enough from those in other groups, for decisions to be made about which, if any, represent an attractive 'target' for the marketing effort.

SEGMENTATION APPROACHES

The means by which a market can be segmented are many and various. Perhaps the simplest and clearest of all is gender: males can be considered one segment and females another. But given that this simply divides the global population roughly in two, it isn't of much practical use, beyond that of demonstrating the principle. Another obvious segmentation factor is age. We can divide males into say, age bands of 0 to 5 years, 6 to 9, 10 to 13, 14 to 17, 18 to 25, 26 to 35, 36 to 50, 51 to 65, 66 to 75, etc. And if we further mix this with a geographical segmentation, for example males aged 18 to 25 living in London (or another large UK city), then we are starting to make some progress.

You can quickly devise segments based on these objective descriptors, and much can be gleaned on this basis, but such blunt facts as gender, age and geography don't reveal enough information on their own to make judgements about a segment. To these simple attributes therefore, marketers have learned to add much richer analytical factors. Perhaps the most famous (or infamous) marketing segmentation approach is the demographic one which classifies people into social grades (A, B, C1, C2, D and E) according to their occupation and its inferred income and lifestyle choices.

WHO SAID IT . . .

"I notice increasing reluctance on the part of marketing executives to use judgment; they are coming to rely too much on research, and they use it as a drunkard uses a lamp post, for support rather than for illumination."
– David Ogilvy

Other segmentation approaches include: geo-demographic, psychographic, mediagraphic, and behavioural.

The geo-demographic approach looks at neighbourhood and house type rather than broad geographical location, to infer lifestyle and buying behaviour (ACORN is a well known proprietary service which takes this approach, making in-depth analyses of people's lives based on the size and type of house in which they live).

The psychographic approach examines instead people's mental worlds, taking factors such as lifestyle choice, personality type, values and motivation as the data. One such model describes ten different shopper 'types' ranging from Convenience Shopper to Individualistic Shopper, through to Socially Conscious Shopper and Shop-Til-I-Drop Shopper. Another psychographic model called VALS2, which has echoes of Maslow, divides people according to their broad orientation towards 'principle', 'status', or 'action', with further sub-divisions including types as diverse as 'Status-oriented Strugglers' (with ambition but minimal resources) and 'Principle-oriented Fulfilleds' (with high ideals and abundant resources).

A mediagraphic approach draws conclusions from analysis of media consumed, including newspapers read and purchased, preferred TV channels and so on, building up a picture directly reflective of the media itself, recalling Marshall McCluhan's famous remark: 'the medium is the message'.

A behavioural approach by contrast gets down to the nitty gritty of what people actually buy and consume, as well as their brand loyalty, and their propensity to adopt innovative products. One loyalty model describes four levels of customer loyalty, from Switchers (easily tempted to alternative brands by price, features, offers or advertising messages) through to Hard-core Loyalists who zealously stick with one brand choice.

A further behavioural model describes customers' attitudes to innovative products. Proposed by E. M. Rogers in his 1995 book *Diffusion of Innovations*, it has become the classic model of the relationship between the market and innovation. Rogers described five groups and put a percentage figure on their prevalence in the marketplace. Innovators (2.5% of the market) are described as risk-taking, affluent and educated. They are always at the leading edge of the zeitgeist, creating trends as well as adopting them. Early Adopters (13.5%) are open to buying new products early after launch and they influence others. The Early Majority (34%) follow only after early product problems have been sorted (they would for example have purchased a second-generation e-reader). The Late Majority (34%) are older, more traditional and more sceptical of innovation. They will join the trend, but only once it is very well established. Laggards (16%) are much more conservative and suspicious of new trends.

It is not the actual number of categories in the model or the percentages attributed to them which are significant to marketers, but the principle that a relatively small number of people will lead the adoption of innovative products, a larger number will follow swiftly, and a larger number still will form the bulk of the eventual market. The marketer can therefore decide which group to target, which will in turn influence what products to bring to market, and how to do so.

The segmentation approaches I'm describing here are focused on the consumer marketplace, but the same principles and many of the same tools, with nuanced variations, apply to the business market.

FROM SEGMENTATION TO TARGETING

Dividing a market into meaningful segments is a vital step, but you then need to take a further step: to assess the identified segments in order to decide if it is likely to be profitable to target one or more them. In other words you have to pick which segments are attractive to your company. These have to be hard-nosed questions, with the answers coming from the maximum amount of factual data that can be sourced. Does the segment demonstrate past and present potential sales which give some indication that it will offer sales and profits in the future? Does the segment have the potential for growth, or is it fully-mature or in decline? Is the segment overwhelmed by competitors already? How high or challenging are the barriers to entry, or is it a segment that the company already inhabits in some form? Does the segment have some unsatisfied needs or wants which your company is distinctly in a position to meet? These and more questions ensure that the marketer makes maximum use of the segmentation-targeting process.

From the broad market of, for example, 'everyone in the USA who needs a family car', the segmentation-targeting process can focus the company on parts of the market which are likely to achieve sustainable profit for the company. It is really a process of focus. The whole market is divided into segments. The segments are examined. The most promising one or more are selected as targets on which to train one's marketing resources.

I said earlier that the era of mass marketing is dead, but of course it's not really that clear cut: vestiges of that time remain. In fact adherence to the strategy of mass marketing (also called Undifferentiated Targeting) is still a valid strategy for some very large brands with a strong high street presence (either with their own store or with a ubiquitous product presence). The choice of ways to target a market is really a continuum, with the Undifferentiated approach at one end, as the following figure shows. In undifferentiated markets the mass approach remains an appropriate one, but for more differentiated, concentrated and niche markets you need an increasingly differentiated approach to marketing.

Arguably the ideal is a marketing programme tailored to each customer: which a mere decade ago would have sounded unachievable, but which in the digital age is increasingly common practice. Amazon do it all the time, and it's far from being alone. In a sense brands like Amazon straddle the entire continuum. The 'Amazon' brand is a mass market brand (we've all heard of it) yet its vast array of products is highly differentiated to the point of being niche (individual books and other products which include the obscure and the minority interest as well as the 'hits'), whilst its email marketing to existing customers is tailored to an extraordinary extent, with recommendations based on previous buying patterns.

Mass market to customised market

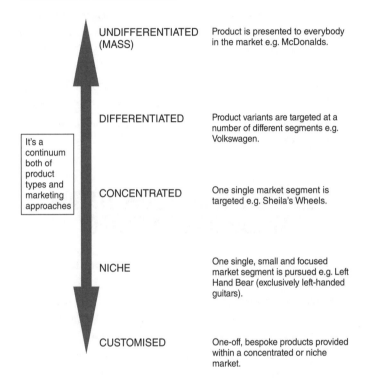

UNDIFFERENTIATED (MASS)	Product is presented to everybody in the market e.g. McDonalds.
DIFFERENTIATED	Product variants are targeted at a number of different segments e.g. Volkswagen.
It's a continuum both of product types and marketing approaches		
CONCENTRATED	One single market segment is targeted e.g. Sheila's Wheels.
NICHE	One single, small and focused market segment is pursued e.g. Left Hand Bear (exclusively left-handed guitars).
CUSTOMISED	One-off, bespoke products provided within a concentrated or niche market.

TAKING A POSITION IN THE MARKET

Positioning is a massive buzz word in the fields of marketing (although it's not a new idea, having been conceived by Al Ries and Jack Trout in the early 1970s) but it's a term that is often misunderstood. A product or brand's 'position' refers to how it is perceived in the mind of the market, *relative* to competing products or brands. It's the word 'relative' that is most important. A brand's position is not absolute and static but will always be perceived in relation to others.

Taking a 'position' is one of the key acts of marketing, and it can be critical to the success or failure of your product. We will examine positioning in more detail in the next chapter.

SIX STEPS FROM SEGMENTATION TO MARKETING STRATEGY

To summarise the journey, as a marketer you have to:

1. Analyse the total potential market for your company's products and services and identify the various segments within the market.
2. Make decisions about the relative attractiveness of different segments.
3. Select one or more segments to target.
4. Research and analyse the perceptions of audiences within the segments about other brands already active in those segments.
5. Choose a position within the target segments that is available, appropriate, credible and potentially profitable.
6. Build a brand marketing strategy (more on marketing strategy and planning later).

TARGET SEGMENTS ARE MADE OF REAL PEOPLE

In the end your 'target segments' aren't theoretical abstracts. They are people. Folk like you and me. Or unlike you and me. But always real, living people with individual needs, wants, desires, anxieties, and dreams. It's easy to forget that fact when you're wading through research and strategy documents. It is people not segments who make buying choices. Much marketing literature refers to buyers' 'decisions' but I prefer to say 'choices' because it's a reminder that much buying behaviour (although voluntary of course) is not governed by rational thought but by emotion.

Buyers of products or services (who may or may not be the end-user) are influenced by a host of factors which can be broadly divided into the internal (personality, health, age, values, resources, ambitions, anxieties etc.), and the external (family, friends, peers, societal trends, the media etc.).

With so many influences upon an individual, and with so many brand messages flying around, and so many products and services available, you might wonder how anyone ever makes a buying choice that is anything other than random. Marketers are very used to the idea of the misery of choice: in which a potential customer can become confused, paralysed like a rabbit the glare of headlights, and ultimately discouraged from purchase.

So how do buyers choose what to buy? It is conventional wisdom to say that buyers follow a stepped process, which is usually described as follows:

1. Potential buyer *identifies their need or problem* (ranging from the trivial urge for a chocolate treat, to the much more substantial need to buy a car or to book a holiday).
2. Potential buyer *carries out information search* (sees what's available to meet the need).
3. Potential buyer *evaluates the alternatives on offer* (Crunchie or Mars? Pacific cruise or trip to Paris?).
4. Potential buyer *makes decision* and becomes actual buyer.
5. Buyer makes some kind of *post-purchase evaluation* which influences future purchasing decisions, and which may influence other potential buyers.

It's easy to knock this model as being too rational and logical, when there is much research to indicate (and we know anyway if we're honest with ourselves) that we don't behave rationally when it comes to our buying behaviour. So do we really identify a need or a problem before we act? Do we really carry out an information search and evaluate all the alternatives on offer? Well not in the strictest sense of course, but even if one takes the simple chocolate bar purchase the model still helps to explain what is going on.

Let's say we happen to be standing on a tube station platform. We aren't thinking about chocolate, but it's a couple of hours since we've eaten, and there are all those chocolate bars temptingly laid out before us. Suddenly we have developed a 'need'. Most of the popular brands are on display (it takes only a couple of seconds to carry out that 'information search'). Those brands on display form what's called our 'awareness set'. Clearly we can't buy something if it isn't there. But there's another subtle marketing truth evident in this example: perhaps there is a brand of chocolate in the display which we are not familiar with. A new brand perhaps. Superficially it has as much chance of being noticed and purchased as all the other bars. In reality of course we may not even actually 'see' it (because it is unfamiliar to us).

We quickly 'evaluate' what's on offer (perhaps prompted by the memory of the amusing TV commercial we happened to see on the TV on the previous evening, featuring a gorilla playing the drums), and we choose a bar of Cadbury's Dairy Milk. We buy.

The whole process has taken perhaps one minute in total, probably less. We may wolf down this bar, or savour it piece by piece along our tube journey, or even save it for later (enjoying the anticipation). Something inside us feels good. CDM we think happily to ourselves (well I do anyway, you might choose something else) really is the best chocolate bar. We might even allow ourselves a little smile which indicates our 'post-purchase evaluation'.

But chocolate bars and cars are not the same, and we respond to them very differently.

WHO YOU NEED TO KNOW
Phil Knight

Among the top 25 wealthiest people in the USA, Phil Knight is the now semi-retired co-founder and Chairman of Nike Inc.

Studying for his MBA at Stanford at the beginning of the 1960s Knight wrote a paper called '*Can Japanese sports shoes do to German sports shoes what Japanese cameras did to German cameras?*' which in effect became the founding document of his extraordinarily successful global brand. Selling his first imported running shoes from the back of a van taught Knight the gritty reality of sales as well as marketing, and the rest of the Nike story is brand legend. Turning the sports shoe from a low involvement practical purchase into an emotionally charged must-have, badged with the Nike swoosh (probably the world's most recognised logo after Coca Cola's) Knights became both a marketing hero and globalisation villain: Nike is one of the brands most frequently criticised for 'sweatshop' labour practices in developing countries.

LOW, MEDIUM AND HIGH INVOLVEMENT

One way that marketers look at the buyer's relationship to the product is to consider 'level of involvement' which refers to the amount of effort that a buyer is prepared to put in to fulfilling their need. A need is a gap between the state the buyer is in now (let's say hungry) and the state they want to be in (let's say full). The out-of-nowhere desire for a bar of chocolate is quick and easy to satisfy (assuming you have the money in your pocket) and it doesn't demand much effort of any kind, physical, mental or emotional. We call that a low-involvement purchase. Buying the usual brand of pet food, or any other every-day purchase is also low-involvement.

Less frequent purchases, such as buying a new steam iron for example, might be considered medium-involvement. It isn't life changing. It doesn't cost a fortune. But it is something that will be used daily for a couple of years, perhaps more. We want one that will function well and be pleasant to use.

Buying a car is obviously much more demanding, so we call that high-involvement. The process may be much less frequent (although not necessarily since we may keep a £30 steam iron for many more years than a £20 000 car), almost certainly more complex, probably much more time-consuming, and will carry a higher financial risk.

With low-involvement purchases the whole step process can be over in seconds, but with high-involvement purchases the process not only takes longer but is more vulnerable to interruption and disruption.

However, our level of involvement isn't just a factor of rational influences like financial risk. Buyer involvement increases with any purchase relating to self-image or social status (including cars, but also clothes, cosmetics, even things as varied as books and mobile phones which are on-display to others). Involvement also increases with the degree of pleasure that the purchase might offer (so choosing holidays is high-involvement, but so is choosing a DVD to rent or a concert to attend).

You may notice an interesting correlation between the involvement level of a particular product or category and the way in which marketers promote them. Low-involvement products, such as convenience foods, are frequently promoted through mass-market, low-involvement, media and marketing activity, such as TV and radio commercials. High-involvement products such as cars also appear in TV commercials, but the brand and product awareness job being done on the TV is supplemented by extensive use of high-involvement media (from brochures, to websites, to press advertising and extensive use of PR to gain positive and detailed reviews).

INFORMATION SEARCH

Once the need is identified the customer starts to search. Sometimes they might just search their memory ('My last dishwasher was a Miele/Bosch/Something and that lasted ten years without problems, so I'll definitely look at those,'). Sometimes they'll lock straight into the influences of peers or of marketing activity ('My friend Simon seems to love his new iPad, and it does look pretty funky in the TV commercials, so perhaps I'll have a look at one instead of a netbook'). Sometimes brand loyalty will limit the information search to looking within the offerings of one brand (many car buyers can become fiercely loyal over many years).

Buying insurance products doesn't demand high emotional involvement, but it is complex enough to be considered a high-involvement purchase. In the past we have traditionally relied on trusted brokers to find us a good insurance deal from a range of providers, or we have formed a trusting relationship with an insurance 'rep' visiting our homes once a year. Today we are more likely to do our insurance information search online, a trend which has been fuelled by the dramatic rise of the aggregator (comparison) website.

And if we are choosing a hotel for a city break or business trip, many of us will use the concept of crowd-sourcing to do our information search, reading the customer reviews on sites such as TripAdvisor.

THE AWARENESS SET AND EVALUATION

If you don't know something exists you cannot consider it. So the marketer's challenge is always to ensure that their brand, product or service is within our awareness. Once you are aware of a product though, you can evaluate it against the other possibilities. The way you evaluate depends a great deal on your influencing factors. If you have limited money to spend you will look at cheaper options, although you might flirt with the fantasy of the more expensive possibilities. It's for this reason of course that many brands offer entry-level products which can open up the brand to customers who have less money to spend (such as the BMW Series 1). You may look for certain features on your hypothetical dishwasher, to suit your family's needs. You may of course evaluate in one way (brand loyalty) and pretend to evaluate in another. We shoppers are highly skilled at rationalising our decisions.

THE PURCHASING DECISION AND POST-PURCHASE EVALUATION

Evaluation complete you make your purchase decision (or choice). It is quite possible that the choice was made long ago, long before the need even arose, based upon a host of influences. It is also possible for the buyer to remain unaware of the real reasons why they have made their particular choice.

Post-purchase feelings can vary from disappointment, if the product fails to perform, or if family or friends are unimpressed, through to simple satisfaction and even delight (which in turn can lead to the customer becoming an advocate and influencing others).

With high-involvement purchases there is an interesting psychological factor at work, which influences our evaluation. Psychologists describe the uncomfortable state of cognitive dissonance which refers to a conflict between our actions and our thoughts and feelings. If we spend a lot of money on something and we know rationally that we have spent unwisely we find ourselves in this state of cognitive dissonance, and our strong human tendency is to look for more information which supports our decision. We look, in other words, for things to make us feel better. It's part of the reason why car companies provide lavish brochures full of product detail and lifestyle images: they are as important after the purchase as they are prior. Of course if we can't rid ourselves of our psychological discomfort this way, then instead we may noisily disassociate ourselves from the brand: which is a massive challenge to marketers in the age of Twitter and other social media.

Cognitive dissonance can be avoided by skilled marketers by following the simple rule of thumb of not over-promising, and by giving customers opportunities to try the product before purchase. An unhappy customer is potentially hugely damaging.

WHAT YOU NEED TO READ

▶ For a detailed explanation of the VALS2 (Values and Lifestyles 2) psychographic approach to segmentation see www.future.sri.com/vals.

▶ A very approachable introduction to the perspectives of key marketing writers and thinkers, all captured in summary form: *The Marketing Gurus*, edited by Chris Murray, Atlantic, 2006.

▶ Chris Anderson is Editor-in-Chief of *Wired* magazine, the monthly bible of the technorati, whose worldwide bestseller *The Long Tail*, Random House, 2006, is a thrilling explanation of how the rise of the internet has changed marketing forever: putting companies and customers in touch with each other like never before, anywhere in the world.

▶ Customer Relationship Management (CRM) was for a while the great hope of the marketing industry, using detailed data capture and insight to respond to customer buying habits. But CRM receives a persuasively devastating critique in Frederick Newell's book *Why CRM Doesn't Work*, Bloomberg, 2003.

▶ The Chartered Institute of Marketing is the UK's professional body for marketers, with a comprehensive and widely recognised education and training programme. Offering marketing qualifications at several levels, the CIM also acts as a useful portal into the world of contemporary professional marketing theory and practice and research: www.cim.co.uk.

IF YOU ONLY REMEMBER ONE THING

No business can market to everybody, so segmenting the market and selecting targets carefully is crucial to success.

CHAPTER 4
BRANDING

WHAT IT'S ALL ABOUT

- ► The rise of brand and branding
- ► Brand and the creation of meaning
- ► Brand as a key differentiator in the market
- ► Beyond brand to Lovemarks
- ► Brand positioning

In the early literature on marketing, including the first edition of Kotler's *Marketing Management* in 1967, there is barely any mention of the word 'brand', and where it is mentioned it is described in somewhat mechanistic or static terms. Forty years ago, even at the height of mass-market advertising, brand was just a descriptor for the 'properties' owned by a company made up of their recognisable goods and services and the names and trademarks that went with them. Brand, in a sense, was just a system of badging a product: the value still lay in the product itself and the company's ability to sell it. Things are different now.

BRAND IN THE BOARDROOM

Brand's status and influence in the boardroom has risen. Not many years ago (up to the late 1990s and even beyond) the person in the company with the lead responsibility for generating profit by getting customers to part with money in exchange for goods was most like to be called the Sales Director. Gradually many of those directors were given an extra element to their role, and became Sales & Marketing Director. As time moved on the Marketing Director became the lead, often with the Sales Director reporting to them. Somewhere in the management tier there were frequently Brand Managers, whose jobs were less concerned with the topic of brand as we are about to explore it, but more with the day to management of the marketing and sales effort relating to discrete collections of products.

But in recent years, since the turn of the century approximately, there has been a marked shift. In many companies the Marketing Director has been joined on the board, or even replaced, by the Brand Director. In other slightly more cautious companies the Marketing Director is closely supported by a Head of Brand or something similar.

But what is brand and why has its star risen so? Brand is not (and this is where confusion often creeps in) fundamentally about logos, brand names or brand-advertising campaigns. Those things play a part, but they are not the brand in themselves.

WHO YOU NEED TO KNOW
Seth Godin

The popular hero of hip modern marketers, Godin's books are short, punchy, opinionated and fantastically popular. Eschewing the academic or corporate attitude to marketing, Godin treats the whole thing as a wild adventure. From his landmark 2002 book *Purple Cow* (arguably the first genuinely pop culture marketing book and certainly the bestselling book on the topic of the noughties) through to the provocatively titled *All Marketers Are Liars* (and several more), Godin is always trying to persuade businesses to be 'remarkable', crucially through the telling and bringing to life of great (and authentic) stories. Invigoratingly direct and often very funny, Godin has done much to make the concept of brand as meaning understood on a wide scale.

BRAND AS A SET OF MEANINGS

Brand is defined most simply as being a set of meanings that consumers, customers (in fact any members of all a company's audiences) carry around in their heads and hearts. To put it another way, a product's or company's or individual's brand can be said to be the sum total of all the things that people think, feel, suspect, imagine, believe, wish, and say about it.

In Chapter 3 we looked at 'positioning' and saw that this too is concerned with meaning (we used the word perception). But where positioning is a relative concept, in that it refers to perceptions in relation to other, competing products and services (this thing is cheaper than that competitor, or of better quality than the other competitor), brand might be said to be more absolute. Brand is less concerned with the shifting sands of relative positioning, and more concerned with the creation and transmitting of meanings which will draw customers to it.

It's not difficult to test the 'brand as meaning' concept. Take any well known brand from any sector, write its name on a piece of paper and ask a number of people to tell you the words or phrases that comes into their minds when they see the name. The results reveal three important truths. First, if there is general agreement on the words and phrases, or at least the meanings behind them, then you can consider your test brand to be a 'strong' one. Strong in the sense that its meanings are small in number, coherent, and understood and shared by different people.

One of my favourite tricks at conferences and workshops is to do this exercise with a large audience, having them shout out the words that they associate with a couple of very famous brands. To underline my point with a flourish I take care to write down the 'meanings' of the brands on paper beforehand and to hand these in a sealed envelope to a member of the audience.

One example is the British department store John Lewis. Over and over again, with audiences across the UK, four key meanings are identified for this brand: quality, service, value, and partnership (the latter referring to the company's mutual ownership structure). Those of course are the words that I have written and sealed in an envelope. This party piece hasn't failed yet. This not only proves the point that John Lewis has managed to get its audiences to absorb and believe a small and powerfully consistent set of meanings, but it also helps to explain why this store is so much loved by its regular customers.

WHO SAID IT . . .

"People make decisions big and small based on just one thing: the lie we tell ourselves about what we're about to do."
– Seth Godin

STRONG DOESN'T NECESSARILY MEAN POSITIVE

By careful design or through philosophical coincidence, but happily for John Lewis, their brand meanings are it seems perfectly in tune with the zeitgeist. In his 2005 book *FAQs on Marketing* Kotler says, 'Customers are most concerned with quality, service and value'. Way to go John Lewis!

Interestingly (and somewhat spoiling my conference party trick) John Lewis has recently started to be much more explicit about its set of meanings and now overtly says: 'Never Knowingly Undersold . . . on quality, on price, and on service'.

This store's brand is therefore not only very strong but also very positive. Being a strong brand is not enough. As BP, Toyota, Tiger Woods, FIFA, Rolls Royce and others have discovered in the few months during which this book was written. A strong brand, BP being the most acute example here can slip from positivity whilst retaining its strength, arguably putting it in the worst position of all (strong/negative, otherwise known as infamy).

The challenge for new brands is to build strength and positivity at the same time, rising from obscurity to positive fame. By contrast the challenge for established and admired brands is to maintain the positive meanings through their behaviour and their relationships with customers. The immense challenge for some brands is to drag themselves somehow from the strong/negative position to something more positive. This is perhaps most starkly seen with nations (which are becoming more and more concerned with brand, because they know that their set of brand meanings has a direct effect on their prosperity and prospects). Afghanistan, tragically, is a very strong brand (famous everywhere with its name immediately evocative of strong visual images), but its set of meanings is immensely negative. Changing the meanings of Afghanistan or indeed any country has more to do with policy making than with marketing of course: but it has everything to do with the mental and emotional power of brand.

Brand strength and positivity

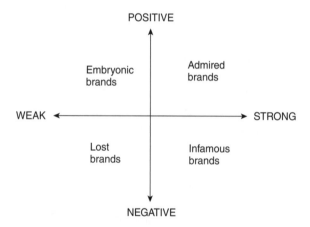

MEANING CHANGES WITH BEHAVIOUR NOT JUST COMMUNICATIONS

In the next chapter we look at marketing communications, one of the many aspects of which is known as Crisis Communications: that sub-set of Public Relations which kicks into action when a brand is in trouble. A brand with problems (a product or service problem for example) certainly needs to communicate with its public, rather than adopt a head-in-sand stance to run for cover, and it's true that the way a brand communicates when it is in crisis can lessen or worsen its problems. Saying 'Sorry' is generally a good thing. Ultimately however it is not communications but behaviour which heals a wounded brand in the long run: and they can be healed. A much admired sportsman who has fallen from grace can rebuild positive meanings, but through behaviours adopted rather than communications. What brands *do* is always much more powerful than what they *say*.

For a brand like BP, the road is a much longer one and the penance required to rebuild positive meaning is much higher: but it is a penance undoubtedly worth paying, because BP know very well the value that lies in its brand.

BRAND AS VALUE

Talk of creating positive meanings may sound soft-centred rather than hard-edged, but you have to remember that positive meanings translate into real value for a company, and damage to those meanings results in a loss of value.

Interbrand is a global brand advisory firm that has pioneered the practice of calculating the financial value of leading brands. Their annual listing of the top ten most valuable brands always makes fascinating reading, and comparing the figures from different years shows trends in technology and in culture being reflected directly by brand success.

In the 2010 listings, Coca-Cola remains at the top of the rankings, with a staggering 'brand' value of over 70 billion dollars. According to Interbrand, technology companies like IBM, Microsoft, Google and Intel owe a huge part of their success to the value in their 'brand', as do other top ten performers like Disney and McDonald's.

Together the brand value of the top ten is estimated at substantially in excess of 400 billion dollars! No wonder these brands invest so heavily in shaping and controlling every brand message (from visual, to aural, to experiential) that they give out: because they know in the end it is their 'brand' which makes them world class businesses.

The next ten in the rankings were Toyota, Mercedes, Gillette, CISCO, BMW, Louis Vuitton, Apple, Marlboro and Samsung.

Despite the vast billions of dollars attributed to brand equity in studies like Interbrand's, such figures don't appear in company accounts, because their measurement is ultimately subjective and hard to prove by conventional accounting measures. Nevertheless the reality of a brand as having financial value is immediately apparent whenever a major one changes hands. When Kraft Foods bought the British chocolate manufacturer company Cadbury in 2010 for $18,900,000,000 the American giant wasn't really buying production facilities or stock, or even expertise: it was buying one of the world's best-loved set of brand meanings. How well Kraft nurtures that brand meaning over time remains to be seen.

And when Rolls Royce's brand reputation was damaged in the same year by a series of problems with its Trent 900 engines, most dramatically in an incident on an Airbus A380 super jumbo flown by Qantas in which an engine partially disintegrated, all three brands suffered immediate and substantial share price falls.

The financial value of brands is immediately apparent on the high street too. The UK street price for an entry level generic PC-laptop is approximately £300. The entry level Apple MacBook is approximately £800. That £500 difference in a sense represents the value of the Apple brand.

THE CHARACTERISTICS OF SUCCESSFUL BRANDS

Strong and positive brands come in every shape and size. Brand success is not defined solely by turnover or even by profit, because these are only ever snapshots of a business. A one-person enterprise can achieve 'brand success' on its own terms, just as much as a global brand. Brands of every kind can be said to have four observable characteristics.

Successful brands have a tendency to be *Authentic*, which is to say that their brand promise will tend to be based on reality rather than fantasy. They are true to themselves in other words. McDonald's for example doesn't make exaggerated claims in any of its advertising about its food or its in-store experience. We could possibly level at the brand that the burgers look a little more enticing in the ads than they do in reality: but the gap isn't a huge one. They've never claimed to be a cordon bleu experience. McDonald's can therefore be said (whether you happen to like it or not) to be an 'authentic' brand. They dallied for a while with health food messaging but have moved away from this, for the simple reason that the audience saw it as in-authentic and it therefore worked against the brand rather than in its favour.

Successful brands have a strong tendency to being highly *Distinctive*. In his 2003 book *Purple Cow* Seth Godin talks about the critical importance of 'being remarkable'. As Godin articulates so simply, consumers have a surfeit of available choices and a shortage of available time to make those choices. So the brand that stands out (a purple cow as opposed to a brown cow) gets noticed. Godin isn't pleading for novelty for its own sake but for brands to create differentiated product and service offerings which meet needs and wants in new and engaging ways.

Successful brands tend to tell *Compelling* stories. In other words great brands know that whilst facts are dull and hard to remember, by contrast stories, myths, legends, jokes, character, drama, are all stimulating, emotionally engaging and memorable. Richard Branson's Virgin brand owes a great part of its success to the founder's own hunger for adventure and ability to translate that into newsworthy narrative. The Innocent drinks brand endlessly tells the story of its origin at a music festival at which it asked customers to indicate (by choosing between two marked bins to dump their empty bottle) whether they should give up and go back to work, or dedicate themselves to creating a smoothie company. Brand stories can cover any topic. Sometimes they are boastful, sometimes self-deprecating, sometimes technical, sometimes emotional. What the great brands' narratives have in common is that they tap into the human love of narrative, which is turn part of our innate desire to make meaning.

Finally, successful brands are most likely to be built on a platform of *Excellence*, which is to say that companies which make product or service promises which are not kept, tend to be exposed quite quickly. Profits can be achieved over the short term, but the brand will not build strong positive meanings which foster customer loyalty.

WHO SAID IT . . .

"A brand for a company is like a reputation for a person. You earn reputation by trying to do hard things well."

– Jeff Bezos

AN ANCHOR IN THE MIND

It's a fact of human cognition that, with our limited mental capacity, we find it difficult to hold contradictory beliefs. We like things to be black or white in other words, and we have trouble with grey. Furthermore, once we have adopted a belief about something, our responses become biased towards that belief. We tend to notice and to gather up data which supports our core belief, and to dismiss, or even fail to notice, information which undermines or contradicts that belief. Which is why, if we are in a happy long-term relationship we tend to overlook our partner's human flaws.

We do much the same with brands, and it is this which makes them so powerful. It is why one person will simply not countenance wearing any training show but Nike, and another would rather go barefoot than have the swoosh-logo anywhere near them. It is why many Blackberry users find the notion of switching to another smartphone brand almost inconceivable. And so on.

This means that almost anything that Nike or Blackberry does will be of positive interest to their adherents. To a point. If either brand betrays its trust by being inauthentic, or failing to achieve excellence, then it is put under test. Because of our natural inclination to filter out the bad news about our beliefs, most minor failures will not damage the brand too much (at least amongst those who already have the brand 'anchored' in their psyche), but a continuous run of negative messages can have a cumulative effect.

LOVEMARKS, THE FUTURE BEYOND BRANDING

There aren't many advertising agencies that are household-name brands in their own right, with a name recognised far beyond the industry within which they work, but one of them is Saatchi & Saatchi. Relatively few lay people will be able to identify much of this firm's work without prompting, but many will know that they are a big agency that makes famous ads for big brands.

Saatchi & Saatchi, interestingly, has been repositioning itself over the last several years, from being an 'ad agency' to being an 'ideas company'. There isn't room here to go into what they mean by that, but it is a process which has been helped in no small part by the remarkable success of two books (and a global online community) created by the firm's CEO Worldwide, Kevin Roberts.

Roberts' *Lovemarks* model, and his two books on the subject *Lovemarks: the future beyond brands* and its sequel *The Lovemarks Effect* have become influential bestsellers and Lovemarks has become a powerful brand in its own right.

Roberts' thesis is simple but it has given rise to a branding model which has been seized upon with enthusiasm by brand-oriented businesses organisations from the tiniest local enterprise to global corporations. The Lovemarks model says, in essence, that companies only have two tools to make use of in the struggle to make their brands engage customers: respect and love.

One of these is uncontroversial. Respect refers to rationality, to what people 'think' about a company, product or service. But the other, love, is still oft considered, in the corporate world, to be a step too far in acknowledging the importance of emotion. Love refers of course to what people 'feel' rather than what they think. The combination of the two factors results in the following matrix. In the bottom right corner lie faddish products which might make a temporary emotional impact but which fail to stick (one-off Christmas hit toys, some pop stars and TV shows, some fashion products and so on). In the bottom left corner are commodities which

have no emotional or intellectual resonance but are purchased because they are cheap or convenient. In the top
left corner sit the conventional brands which have earned
our respect: brands that we are aware of, understand,
probably trust, and of which we 'think' well.

Lovemarks (from Kevin Roberts)

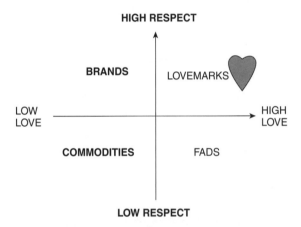

Top left is a good place to be. But top right is the place
of Lovemarks, and for Roberts at least is clearly an ideal.
This is the place reserved for brands which people not
only respect but with which they have formed an emotional bond. One person's Lovemark might of course be
another's brand or fad: but that doesn't undermine the
appeal of the model, or the ambition, particularly to new
and ambitious brands.

Occupying the Lovemarks space is said to offer three
specific benefits:

▶ forgiveness when things go wrong;

▶ 'loyalty beyond reason', allowing the brand to innovate and develop with greater confidence that its audience will follow it;

▶ much less sensitivity to price (meaning the Lovemark can charge more).

Lovemark status is said to be achievable through specific behaviours:

▶ creating 'mystery' (i.e. narratives which engage and involve the audience);

▶ utilising 'sensuality' (operating through all senses rather than the conventional brand tendency to depend upon the visual);

▶ fostering 'intimacy' (by treating customers as individuals).

WHO SAID IT . . .

"People will only respond when you touch their own personalities, dreams and desires – when you understand what attracts them. Never has being in tune with consumers been so important."

– Kevin Roberts

FROM BRAND TO BRAND POSITIONING

We touched briefly upon positioning in Chapter 3 and we will look in more detail at the concept here. Positioning is related to the concept of brand, but whereas brand might be described as an 'absolute' set of meanings or perceptions, positioning is a much more relative concept, referring to perceptions of a brand in relation to perceptions of a competitor.

The second most important (and uncomfortable) truth about positioning is that it is very much a two-sided affair: a brand can 'claim' any position it thinks is appropriate, but because everything depends on market perception, that desired position is by no means guaranteed. There is a very real sense in which brand position has to be won, or earned. And to add further challenge to the marketer, the market itself is rarely, if ever, static. The market shifts constantly in all kinds of unpredictable ways and what appears to be a rock-solid position today may seem like a very wobbly one tomorrow. British Airways positioned itself for many years as 'The World's Favourite Airline' (based on the fact that it flew more people on more routes than anyone else, and interpreting that somewhat wistfully as meaning that it was better liked than any other airline).

Nevertheless, for all its challenges, the concept of positioning provides a hugely powerful lever to the marketer, providing that a position is chosen that is genuinely available (not already 'owned' by a competitor), appropriate to the brand, credible to the audience, and of course profitable to the company itself. There really is nothing to be gained by taking a position which is distinctive and credible which puts the brand in such a refined place that no profit can be made.

An almost infinite range of positioning approaches are possible, and a few examples will illustrate best.

▶ *Position based on product attributes*: such as Guinness making an epic virtue of the time it takes for a pint of the black stuff to settle.

▶ *Position based on occasions when the product is used*: such as Kit Kat's strong association with taking a well-earned 'break'.

▶ *Position according to the aspirations of the user*: such as Coutt's Bank which is so firmly identified as The Queen's bank.

▶ *Position based on values*: The Co-operative Bank has strongly associated itself with ethical finance.

▶ *Position based on a 'promise'*: such as John Lewis's 'Never knowingly undersold', or FedEx's commitment to getting your package to its destination overnight.

▶ *Position alongside other brands or a whole category*: such as Intel's brilliant 'Intel Inside' campaign which has given a hidden component part the status of a customer-facing brand.

▶ *Position against other brands*: perhaps most famously the car hire firm Avis who since 1962 have consistently claimed 'We try harder' (originally to distinguish themselves from market-leader Hertz).

▶ *Position against a whole category:* such as Apple's 'I'm a Mac' campaign which starkly contrasted the Apple ethos against the whole PC industry.

Because of the constant threat from competition and the shifting of the market, well-established and carefully positioned brands can often find themselves forced to try to re-position. Re-positioning does not mean starting from scratch of course. In fact, if a brand has established a strong position but that position is no longer appropriate then trying to re-position is one of the biggest marketing challenges of all.

WHO YOU NEED TO KNOW
Al Ries

Along with co-author Jack Trout, Al Ries is credited with the creation of the concept of brand positioning, first with a series of legendary articles in *Advertising Age* magazine in 1972 and subsequently the book *Positioning: the battle for your mind.* Ries's reputation remains undiminished today and he has constantly updated and refined his ideas. Ries's core notion is that a product or a service has to be 'positioned' in the mind of the potential customer in such a way that it is perceived as significantly different from its competitors. Ries's idea of positioning became known as the fifth 'P' of marketing (along with Product, Price, Place and Promotion). Ries continues to write and speak, and heads up the consultancy firm Ries & Ries with his daughter and co-author Laura.

BRAND ARCHITECTURE

It is often the case, and often a real challenge for those that have to manage them, that several brands will sit alongside one another in a company's portfolio. Brand Architecture refers to the ways in which companies organise their various brands in relation to each other. It matters for several reasons including: the avoidance of clashes of brands trying to occupy the same position, ensuring that each brand is managed and funded appropriately according to its importance and potential, and to make best use of possible synergies between brands.

Brand architecture as a discipline became important with the rise of FMCG (fast moving consumer goods) marketing, with numerous brands, which to the consumer appear discrete entities, being owned and managed by a relatively small number of companies. One of the discipline's key outputs is that it can reveal when a particular brand is out of sync in some way with a company's broad ambitions and objectives.

There are numerous solutions to the challenge of brand architecture, but three in particular have become well known.

The *monolithic brand* is one in which the brand name and core messages remain constant across the portfolio. Different products will have simple distinguishing names (which sometimes imply relative status) but none are allowed to develop a personality away from the core brand. BMW is a classic example: the entire range of its cars being signified by Series numbers only. The BMW-owned Mini brand (whilst it enjoys some kudos of association with the engineering excellence of its owner) is a completely separate brand.

The *house of brands* is the model most common in the FMCG market. Unilever and Procter and Gamble for example each own and manage large numbers of well known brands, each of which has its own visual identity and brand personality (and in many cases its own brand architecture). The names of the companies behind these brands, whilst not exactly hidden, are nevertheless recessive rather than dominant.

The *branded house* works the other way around, utilising the equity of the central brand to endorse and underwrite the product brands in the portfolio. Virgin is one of the best known companies to adopt this approach, with Virgin brands covering a vast range of markets, from financial services to media to airlines, all carrying the distinctive Virgin identity and its particular personality.

BRAND IDENTITY

At the beginning of this chapter I remarked that brand is not the same as logo: but that's not to say that design doesn't have a huge role to play in branding. The visual identity of a brand is one of its key touchpoints with its audiences, and it is hard to think of a strong brand which doesn't also have a recognisable visual identity. The identity goes beyond the logo itself, to encompass the consistent use of certain typefaces, colours, styles of imagery and other visual 'cues', all of which help to trigger recognition and brand association in the mind of the audience.

The story goes that the iconic Coca Cola bottle (the most recognised brand property in the world) stemmed from a design brief which demanded that even if the bottle were dropped and smashed any single piece of it would be recognisable instantly as being 'Coke'.

Other brands, notably Nike with its 'swoosh' and Orange with its simple orange square, have created visual properties which are so powerful that they operate as triggers without the need for accompanying words or messages. The difference between these two examples is significant however. Whilst Nike instantly triggers a set of meanings centred around concepts like performance and achievement, the Orange square, though recognisable, does not trigger the same consistency of response. And that's not the fault of the logo, but a failing in the brand to maintain its 'meaning set'.

Brand identity is more than just visual. Intel, Microsoft and McDonald's are just three brands which have created 'sound logos' to great effect. Other brands put much effort into creating a distinctive 'tone of voice', and still others use other senses, such as smell. There were rumours for several years of Barclays developing a unique scent which would be noticeable in every branch (apparently intended to convey the feeling that your money was being well looked after).

BRAND EXTENSION AND SUB-BRANDS

When a brand is established and showing signs of either success or distress, many companies start to dream up new brands, sub-brands and brand extensions. The phrase brand extension just describes the phenomenon of a brand being successful in one arena taking its brand name into another. There are real advantages to this move, but also great dangers. Brand success tends to make sense for the company when it makes sense to the customer: when the customer either understands or feels that there is a real connection between the two products which bear the same brand name?

The Polo brand from Ralph Lauren successfully made the jump from clothing to home furnishings. The connections are strong: linen, comfort, New England style. The Arm & Hammer toothpaste brand was a natural extension of the same brand's baking soda product. Virgin is one of the greatest of brand extenders, as we have already seen. But when connections are tenuous brand extensions are likely to be less successful. Virgin Cola is no longer with us, nor Colgate ready meals. Nor bicycles from Smith & Wesson (yes the gun manufacturer).

Brand extension is used all the time as a method of 'protecting' new products in a ruthless marketplace where anonymity can mean quick death. A successful brand extension means one is no longer starting from scratch. But not only is extension a fast-track to launching a new product or service in a new sector, it can also be a very quick way to damage all the good work done to create the original brand.

One of the most famous of all brand extension flops was Coca Cola's introduction of 'New Coke' in 1985. A quarter of a century later this embarrassing failure continues to be recounted and must have done the company untold financial damage in terms of lost sales over the years. Of course the company has successfully introduced other extensions, of several different kinds, but it's never again tried to 'replace' its original product.

BIC Pens tried to produce BIC tights and stockings. The link was disposability. BIC pens are used and thrown away. As are BIC disposable razors. Same for the tights, went the theory. But women didn't want them. There 'seemed' to be a logical connection: but there wasn't any kind of emotional one. Some recent brand extension successes include pet-food producer Iams launching pet insurance (a clear logical/emotional connection?), Starbucks launching a coffee liqueur, and National Geographic cleverly partnering with Google Earth to give the long established National Geographic brand a whole new lease of life.

Another facet of brand extension is the 'sub-brand' which describes a kind of child of the original brand. Again, there are potentially real benefits in giving the new brand a kick-start in the market-place, but there are also dangers. Walkers have had great success with their Sensations sub-brand, but have not done as well with other extensions. Cadbury's opened hot-chocolate shops and then closed them. PG opened tea-shops and then closed them.

WHAT YOU NEED TO READ

▶ For a detailed exploration of the Lovemarks concept, with heaps of case studies, *The Lovemarks Effect: winning the customer revolution*, Kevin Roberts, Powerhouse Cultural Entertainment Books, 2006.

▶ For my personal take on brand and branding, written primarily for small business readers, *Build A Brand In 30 Days*, Simon Middleton, Capstone, 2010.

▶ Looking beyond the business of branding into its psychology and sociology is Rob Walker's accessible book *I'm With The Brand*, Constable 2008.

▶ For daily, authoritative news about brands from all over the world this website from leading brand agency Interbrand is hard to beat: www.brandchannel.com.

▶ For the definitive introduction to the concept of positioning, with over half a million copies in print: *Positioning:The battle for your mind*, Al Ries & Jack Trout, McGraw Hill, 1981.

▶ Wally Olins was a founder of Wolff Olins, perhaps the world's most famous brand identity design firm, and his book *On Brand*, Thames & Hudson 2003 presents a detailed look at branding from the designer's perspective.

IF YOU ONLY REMEMBER ONE THING

A company's or a product's brand is the sum total of what people think and feel about it, and thus the key influencer on customer behaviour.

CHAPTER 5
COMMUNICATING

WHAT IT'S ALL ABOUT

- ▶ Promotion – where marketer and customer meet
- ▶ The difference between push and pull marketing
- ▶ Getting attention and prompting action
- ▶ Getting the right promotional mix
- ▶ The elements of marketing communications

So far we have looked at the central importance of the customer, the necessity of developing products that people want and need, and the discipline of analysing the market environment and segmenting the market. But up to this point we have barely mentioned the part of marketing which to the outsider is often seen as the whole: promotion.

THE SECOND 'P'

Promotion is the second 'P' of marketing's famous 4Ps model of the 'marketing mix' devised in 1960 by the influential Michigan University professor E. Jerome McCarthy (author the influential book *Basic Marketing: A Managerial Approach* which is still in print today). The other Ps are Product, which we have already examined, Place and Price, which we come to in the next chapter). Promotion in the sense we are using it here is rather broader in scope than it sounds. In fact many marketers refer instead to 'marketing communications' or the shorthand 'marcomms'. The terms are synonymous. We will use 'marketing communications' simply because it is more broadly descriptive of the discipline: which involves the strategy and the process by which marketers communicate with audiences.

THE MARKETING COMMUNICATIONS MIX

Traditionally marketing communications falls into four broad disciplines, each of which plays a different role in the overall marcomms picture:

- ▶ Advertising;
- ▶ Public relations (popularly known as PR);
- ▶ Sales promotion;
- ▶ Personal selling.

Since the dramatic rise of the internet the first three of these are just as likely to be carried out 'online' as in the offline world. But of course the digital age has done more than change emphasis, it has changed the rules. The rise of the social networks, from MySpace to Facebook, from Twitter to LinkedIn and all the many others, has not only provided 'new media' in which marketing communications can be carried out, but has also offered new rules of engagement, new etiquette, new norms and mores, new challenges and opportunities, and new language. We will look in detail at the impact of marketing on the digital age in Chapter 8.

But first, some principles.

MARKETING COMMUNICATIONS STRATEGY

Before the marketer begins to communicate they need to be confident not just about what they are communicating, but why: in other words to work from a strategic purpose. Marketing communications is said to have four key objectives (somewhat annoyingly labelled with the mnemonic acronym DRIP).

1. *To differentiate.* The first task of marcomms is to demonstrate to the audience the difference between the company's product and that of competitors.
2. *To remind.* The second task is to nudge those who are already aware of the product, and who may include previous customers, to remind them of its existence and its benefits to them.
3. *To inform.* The third task is to give the audience the information they require in order to take them further along the road to purchase. This includes facts about the product's features and specifications, as well as information about price, location, purchase process, offers and so on.
4. *To persuade.* The fourth task is to try to engage, excite and stimulate the potential customer: to tap into their needs or wants and to make a connection between those needs and the product.

As with most of the models I've described, this is an iterative rather than a linear process. The tasks are intimately
woven together. Part of persuasion is differentiation, and
the need to remind and inform are hard to separate in
the reality of the marketplace.

THE DIFFERENCE BETWEEN THE MARKET AND THE AUDIENCE

The target market, as we have seen, refers to the customers or potential customers: the people who will buy the
product. The target audience on the other hand, refers
to the people with whom we wish to communicate. The
two groups may of course have many people in common,
but that isn't always the case and it is important that you
think of the two groups separately before you think of
the overlaps, because the truth of the matter is that we
rarely make buying choices alone.

When we buy, as in so much of life, we are influenced by
the groups to which we belong, from our family to our
friendship and work groups, community groups, neighbours and so on. These are known as reference groups.
And it isn't just the groups of which we are already
members which exert an influence: the groups which we
would like to be a part of also have a strong effect on our
buying behaviour. If we aspire to be part of the fashion-
able set then perhaps one or two high fashion accessories
will help? If we identify with the romantic and rebellious

brand of Harley Davidson motorcycles, but we are not bikers, then perhaps a Harley T-shirt will have an appeal.

You can see this effect everywhere and it is especially obvious in clothes and other visual markets such as interior design and furnishing. Much harder to observe, by definition, but arguably just as important is the influence of what are known as dissociative groups: those to which we do not wish to belong. We might, for example, dismiss a particular brand of car from our consideration set because, despite its many merits, it somehow gives off the wrong signal about us.

It has been suggested that purchases aren't actually made by individuals at all but by 'decision making units' which consist of five different roles. The *Initiator* starts the process, by identifying a need or want. This could be a child (hence the importance of pester power) or a reviewer, or the consumer herself. The *Influencer* then gives advice or an opinion (and this role may be a shop assistant, a knowledgeable friend, or a website). The *Decider* makes the choice of what to buy, and this role may or may not be played by the consumer. There is evidence that women make most buying decisions in a household, even if men actually make the purchase or use the product. The *Buyer* actually makes the transaction. Finally the *User* (or consumer) gets hold of the product or service. Four out five of those roles can be played by the same person, but the likelihood is that others are involved: which raises another important question for marketers: to whom should we direct our marketing effort?

In the business market the concept of the decision making unit has a more literal reality, in that certain individuals and teams in a company or other organisation will formally be charged with the responsibility of making purchasing decisions.

So the target audience in fact consists of all the individuals and groups of people who influence product choice and purchase. They are many and various, and they range from your child and your grandmother to your work colleague, your boss, to the producers of the TV shows and movies that you watch.

PUSHING AND PULLING IN THE MARKET

As consumers we generally don't spend a huge amount of time pondering how the products that we buy found their way into the shops that we stroll through, or on to the websites that we browse. Now and again we may wonder how a company came up with such an amazing innovation (Dyson AirBlade, Apple iPhone, etc.) or such a delicious new flavour (chocolate with chilli suddenly seems to be all the rage for example): but even when we acknowledge the innovation itself, we rarely think of the marketing process which led the product to the shelf.

We give little thought to this because of where we stand as consumers in the marketing process. We are at the 'pull' end, figuratively pulling the product through the distribution channels (shops, online stores, etc.)

by the act of purchase. And we've been stimulated to make our purchases by a 'pull' marketing communications strategy: a strategy which has focused on us, the customers. In a pull strategy the efforts of the marketer are trained on us, on our needs and our desires.

A 'push' marcomms strategy by contrast, looks down the other end of the telescope. With a push strategy the effort is focused on persuading shops, websites and other intermediaries to stock the product or to provide the service. You frequently see push strategies in hard-edged industrial businesses, and push marketing is the one area where the 'sales rep' still thrives: visiting the retailer with new products, samples, and incentives to stock extra lines or increased numbers. In prescription pharmaceuticals for example, which are only available to the patient via the General Practitioner, the pharmaceutical company's rep is 'pushing' the product to the GP, rather than to the end user.

It is most often true that pull and push strategies work hand in hand, but the balance between them will differ according to the market. Musical instrument manufacturers will advertise directly to enthusiastic readers of, say, guitar magazines: but that 'pull' advertising effort, although the more visible to the consumer, will be much less significant and extensive than the 'push' effort that they undertake with instrument wholesalers and retailers. Publishers too will 'pull' advertise their books to potential readers, but they will put huge promotional effort into 'push' marketing with major bookshops. The producers of fast moving consumer goods (FMCGs) will, once they have become established brands on the supermarket shelves, still put resource and effort into 'push' activity with the supermarket buyers: but the huge bulk of their marketing spend will be focused on encouraging us the shoppers to 'pull'.

Simple push-pull model

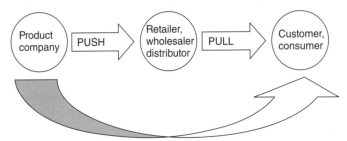

Product company can apply balance of effort and resource towards *pushing* to retailer/distributor/distributor or towards encouraging customer/consumer to *pull*.

OBSTACLES IN THE MARCOMMS PROCESS

It ought to be simple, the marketing communications process. There are, after all, only two principal participants. First there's the company that wants to do some marketing (the *sender*). Then there's the individual in the target audience to whom the company wants to send its message (the *receiver*). And if it were just a simple one-to-one message, like one child speaking to another via two yoghurt pots and a taut piece of string, then marketing communications would be gloriously easy.

The reality however is fraught with difficulties. Part of the problem is the sheer number of people and organisations involved. Here's the usual marcomms process, simplified for our purposes:

1. The company (the maker of the product or provider of the service) has identified its target market and its key messages.

2. The company engages an intermediary such as an advertising agency or PR consultancy, who has expertise in this sort of thing.

3. The agency/consultancy 'encodes' the message into a form that they think will work in appropriate media (a TV commercial, or a press ad, or a blog post, or a press release, or an event). And bear in mind that the encoding process will often involve 'creativity' (an imaginative, seductive, glamorous or perhaps humorous interpretation of the original message). Oh yes, and the actual production of the TV commercial, or the website, will probably involve another set of specialists.

4. The message is sent out using various media channels, from TV to web, etc. (and the choice and booking of media may well involve another specialist company).

5. Some of your target audience (if all your professionals along the way have been doing their job properly) will encounter the message in one form or another, perhaps in more than one

form. I say 'encounter', because that is not the same as 'receive'. *Some* of those who encounter it will receive it (which is to say they will realise it is intended for them and will give it some attention).

6. The receivers (and their numbers depends not only on how well the message has been crafted but on a host of external factors, such as what other messages are flying around that day) then have to *decode* the message. In other words, they have to reverse-engineer the commercial or the event, or the press ad, to figure out what it is you are really trying to tell them. One of the big uncomfortable questions for marketers is: why would they bother?

And that six stage process doesn't take account of everything else that's happening around you. Perhaps there's a big news story which clashes with or simply overwhelms your marketing message. Perhaps there are cultural issues which you haven't thought through and your message is misinterpreted or causes offence. Perhaps your agency creative team is just too bloomin' creative and people just don't 'get' your ad, or they misunderstand it. In the end the effectiveness or otherwise of communications activity comes down to perception: and humans have an annoying habit of not always perceiving things as other humans would like them to.

And then there's the problem of feedback: which is difficult to obtain and difficult to rely on for decision-making.

Your product does well: is it because of your advertising or PR activity? Your product does badly: is it because of your advertising or PR activity?

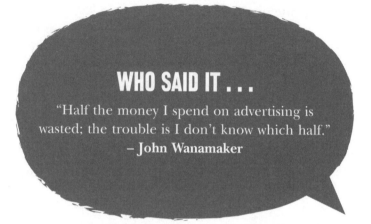

WHO SAID IT . . .

"Half the money I spend on advertising is wasted; the trouble is I don't know which half."
– **John Wanamaker**

FROM GAINING ATTENTION TO PROMPTING ACTION

In the last chapter we looked at a model which describes the buyer's purchasing decision process, which began with said buyer identifying that they have a need or a desire.

A related model, popularly known as AIDA (but more properly called a Hierarchy of Effects model) describes the process by which the marketer needs to communicate with that buyer. It's a useful model, but like most models it has hidden traps if taken too much at face value.

The essential first stage is *Attention*. It is self-evident that you have to gain someone's attention before you can communicate with them. Or is it? There is a strong school of thought, supported by research, that we don't actually pay much attention to marketing messages at all, and that we respond unconsciously to sensory and emotional stimuli, which operate way below our conscious radar. So perhaps 'attention' (which implies awareness) isn't really the issue at all.

The second stage is *Interest*, meaning that once attention is gained we have to stimulate the interest of the potential customer by showing them how the product or service will be of benefit to them, in other words how it will meet their wants and needs.

The third stage is *Desire*, which represents the step in the buyer's mind from recognition that the product will meet their needs to them actually 'feeling' that they wish to purchase it.

The fourth and final stage is *Action*: which requires prompting the actual act of purchase.

You can see all four of these steps played out on almost any piece of direct mail that drops on to your doormat or arrives in your email inbox. From insurance to double glazing, companies will try to grab your attention with a headline offer which sounds amazingly generous or a question which is designed to unsettle you ('Who will care for your loved ones when you've gone?'). They will stimulate your interest by showing how your problem can be solved. They will try to fuel your desire by showing just how your life will be enhanced and by how affordable the product is. And they will call upon you to act with phone numbers, time-limited offers, and straightforward instructions ('Call today: our friendly sales staff are ready to take your order').

As with decisions about push and pull, AIDA presents the marketer with decisions to make about where to spend their money and effort. The four stages of AIDA are most frequently used in combination with each other, but with varying emphasis, and with different techniques.

Gaining attention (which is more or less synonymous with the concept of 'brand awareness') and stimulating interest are frequently carried out with brand advertising, PR and sponsorship, and with trialling. We will look at these approaches in more detail presently, but as a brief example, think of the most recent commercial for a new car that you've seen on TV. There's very rarely an overt attempt to 'sell' you the car. And there will be very little by way of hard facts about the car. The fundamental purpose of the commercial is to gain your attention – to make you aware that the car exists, so that it becomes part of your awareness set.

On the other hand, marketers' efforts to awaken your desire and to prompt you to action tend to be carried out using a different battery of techniques including, as already mentioned, direct mail (DM), as well as sales promotion, direct response (DR) advertising, point of sale (POS), and good old-fashioned personal selling.

An alternative Hierarchy of Effects model known as DAGMAR (define advertising goals for measured advertising results) was devised by Russell Colley in 1961. It's a more brand-focused model, and some will think that it gets closer to describing reality.

The DAGMAR model

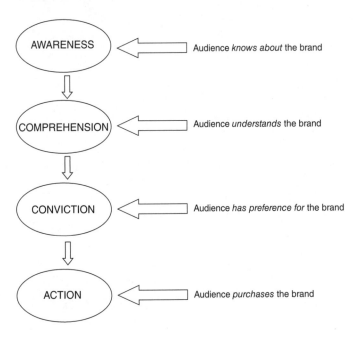

AWARENESS — Audience *knows about* the brand

COMPREHENSION — Audience *understands* the brand

CONVICTION — Audience *has preference for* the brand

ACTION — Audience *purchases* the brand

WHO YOU NEED TO KNOW
David Ogilvy

Probably the most famous advertising man who ever lived, David Ogilvy was born in the UK and emigrated to the USA in 1938. 10 years later he launched the agency that would eventually become the globally renowned Ogilvy & Mather. Ogilvy, a former (highly successful) Aga Cookers salesman who had not written a single advertisement before setting up his agency, went on to become one of the most effective copywriters and ad concept creators in the history of the industry. With an unusual balance of creative flair and analytical commitment to the sales effectiveness of his ads, he was a pioneer of the smart and clever advertising writing style of the 1960s and onwards. Though his milestone book *Ogilvy on Advertising* cannot be considered timeless (it is very much of its era, an era of big-spending mass market communications) it is nevertheless a touchstone for anyone interested in understanding what makes truly great advertising so engaging and so distinct from the banal work that too often surrounds it.

ADVERTISING: NOT DEAD YET

Commentators have been predicting the end of the advertising age for many years. Positioning guru Al Ries wrote a bestseller called *The Death of Advertising and the Rise of PR*. It is undoubtedly true that the advertising industry, as portrayed in its heyday in the hit TV series 'Mad Men', has faced huge challenges over the past two decades in particular.

The rise of PR as a promotional activity has certainly been one of those challenges. But it is technological advance that has put the most pressure on an industry which once believed that creativity of execution combined with a big enough media budget could solve any marketing problem.

Technology, now almost ubiquitous, which allows us to pause and restart programmes, as well as to record them in their entirety, also allows us to skip the ad breaks which were once the battleground of big brand advertising. Newspaper sales have been in steady decline for two decades, so press ads reach fewer people. And, biggest challenge of all, the rise of the internet, which has changed not only our attitudes to advertising as consumers, but the economic models of advertising.

For all the changes though, advertising continues to be a major method by which companies communicate with their audiences. The method has a number of key characteristics:

▶ It is 'paid for', not only in its creation (by copy-writers and art directors in ad agencies, as well as by TV production companies and so on) but in the media required to transmit it (from inter-net pay-per-click advertising through to major TV slots). Media costs are falling in real terms as TV companies and newspaper publishers struggle to keep advertisers on board despite declining audience numbers, but advertising nevertheless remains an enormously expensive route to market.

▶ It almost only ever has an effect through repeti-tion, so advertising tends to be created and shown in 'campaigns' lasting weeks or months. Over the course of a campaign audiences will tend to see an advertisement or broadcast com-mercial several times, with a gradual increase in awareness (which can be followed by a tailing off or irritant effect if the campaign goes on too long or the ad is shown too often). There are exceptions to this rule: the famous '1984' ad announcing the arrival of the Apple Mac computer was shown only once, during the com-mercial break in the Superbowl. But to break the rule you not only need the budget for a major slot (Superbowl) but also complete self-assuredness that your product is exciting enough to make an impact from one advertising outing.

▶ It doesn't give very quick or very reliable feed-back, partly because of the familiarity effect (new brands and products take a while to gain attention) and partly because it is so difficult to attribute sales to specific advertising activity, or to specific elements within that activity.

You can use advertising simply to try to achieve an immediate boost in sales, and you see plenty of advertising, in all kinds of media, that tries to do exactly that. But arguably the ultimate function of advertising, as for marketing in its totality, is to build a brand sustainably rather than simply to achieve the sale, and advertising can contribute to that overall aim in a variety of ways. Advertising can create awareness from scratch, but it can also encourage recognition and recall of products seen in store for example. Advertising is probably at its most effective when it works in combination with other activities, allowing recognition and recall to happen across parallel encounters with the brand.

Advertising is often used to remind consumers about products which have been forgotten or which have become invisible through over-familiarity, and it is used frequently to reposition products. Saying, in effect, 'you thought we were like this, but actually we're now like that'. One of the most recognisable advertising slogans in the history of the industry is also one of the best examples of a repositioning campaign: 'Think you know Spain, think again'.

Because of its sensory and imaginative potential, advertising is a powerful means of achieving differentiation: making a product stand out from the crowd. At the time of writing there was an astonishingly simple TV campaign running for the new MacBook Air: astonishing because without having to labour the point it lets our eyes discover the class-leading thinness of the product. It doesn't even have to tell us that no other laptop or netbook computer can rival this product's thinness: but the confident claim is implicit. There may well be many other measures by which this product does not truly stand out from the crowd: but the point is that the TV commercial has focused on just one very visual element to achieve that differentiation.

Advertising also has a role to play post-purchase. It can reassure customers that their purchase is justified, rewarding their loyalty with the pleasure of seeing an ad of which they approve. The owner of an entry level Series 1 BMW may well get a very real sense of enjoyment and reassurance from seeing a commercial for a much more expensive high-end car from the same manufacturer, cementing loyalty which may in time result in them moving up the 'brand ladder' to buy a more expensive model. Equally, an annoying ad can have a dissociative effect on the recent purchaser and make them quietly resolve never to buy that brand again.

Advertising can inform and educate, and this is particularly important in high-involvement and technically complex purchases for which the customer seeks data, explanation and reassurance as well as inspiration. Complex financial products, some car advertising, ads for technical products such as cameras, often deliver substantial amounts of information about features, but also educate about use.

And lest we forget, advertising can of course just sell stuff. For all its power as a brand awareness tool, or a repositioning tool, a well placed, well crafted ad can prompt purchase of a product or service, from the page, from the TV or radio, or from the page on the internet (whether on a search engine, a social network, or a company website). There is a caveat to this statement though, which is simply that advertising rarely if ever achieves maximum sales on its own. For the reasons which we explored early in this chapter, the process of getting the message to the audience is just too complex and littered with distractions and obstacles, for most advertisements to sell most effectively if they are run purely in isolation, divorced from any other aspect of the marketing mix.

A Google Adwords pay-per-click ad may be so well worded and so well placed through its keywords that it achieves a very high click-through rate from customers who are hot to purchase the product on offer: but the purchase still depends on the experience of the website itself. Further, it is a fact that pay-per-click ads on search engines are less well trusted than the so-called natural or organic listings. It follows that advertising which is 'supported' by natural listings are better trusted and achieve higher click-through. Advertising is still a powerful marketing tool, but the wise marketer will use it in the context of a mix of activity.

FOUR ELEMENTS TO GET RIGHT

To summarise, there are four key areas of advertising to get right in order for it to be a profitable marketing communications investment.

First, the *Audience*. There is no point at all in advertising to the wrong audience. All advertising has wastage built into it, almost by definition. Not everyone who watches the show in which your commercial appears will have a propensity to buy what you are selling, though this is mitigated to some extent by the potential size of the audience. A huge challenge for any advertiser or any agency is the structuring of a campaign that will reach the optimum number of people who fit your customer profile, whilst minimising the wastage on those who don't. There is no such thing as a perfectly targeted campaign in conventional advertising: which is why direct marketing offers a tempting alternative, and why digital media also has great attraction. More on them subsequently.

Second is the *Message* itself. It's become almost an article of faith in advertising that any given ad should only carry one message (often called the single-minded proposition). This tenet grew up, backed to some extent by research, as a foil to the ongoing tendency of clients (the client company of the ad agency that is) to cram a plethora of messages and information into their advertising, to the point that no reader of the ad or viewer of the commercial could possibly be expected to absorb or to respond to what was being thrown at them. Instead, argued the single-minded proposition advocates, ads should tell one story, give one message, powerfully and memorably. Curiously in recent years the tide of opinion on this theme has turned somewhat. Contemporary commentators have argued that psychological research (related to that which indicates that we don't deal with advertising in our conscious mind anyway but rather through 'low-involvement processing') shows that humans are after all quite capable of absorbing complex, multi-layered and 'fuzzy' messages. So the jury might be said to be out on the single-message v. multi-message debate.

Third is the *Creative* aspect of advertising. You don't have to have worked in an ad agency, or even to have watched 'Mad Men' to know that creative interpretation lies at the heart of the advertising industry. The accepted truth about advertising is that simply giving data is not enough and that successful advertising is, almost by definition, that which is also 'creative'. From the classic use of humour (Martians mocking the primitive Earthlings' use of the potato) through to enigmatic drama (surfers waiting for the big wave as a metaphor for the patience required to allow a pint of Guinness to settle), advertising is certainly full of memorable examples of creativity. But creativity is highly (totally?) subjective. Proving that creative advertising sells more or less than less creative work is probably impossible, but so is disproving it. It is generally accepted that there is some correlation between the biggest, longest-thriving consumer brands, and the brands which use creative advertising. But which is cause and which is effect is a much harder question to answer. Oddly enough when clients urge their agencies to be more straightforward in their approach, they are often heard to ask for more of the 'does what it says on the tin' advertising. I say oddly because although it's clear what they mean (less creativity and more factual messaging please) the Ronseal ad campaign that they are referring to was in fact a highly creative interpretation of that brand's promise.

The fourth part of the advertising puzzle is the *Media*. Where you actually put your ads and how often you put them there is a science and an art all of its own. Through a combination of experience and research, a good media specialist can ensure that a campaign operates at maximum effectiveness, reaching the right people, who have the right profile, the right number of times. Big-spending clients traditionally want to enjoy high profile advertising spots, but the media advisor's role is in part to warn against vanity-buying and to lobby for effectiveness instead.

DIRECT RESPONSE ADVERTISING

An important sub-category of advertising is direct response advertising (not to be confused with direct marketing, below). Direct response advertising, whether in press, online or on TV (DRTV), is much less concerned with brand building than other forms of advertising. Direct response is about selling. There tends to be less 'creativity' and more directness of tone, and plenty of clarity in the call to action (which may not always be to actually purchase, but often to arrange for a quotation, for new windows or a stairlift perhaps). Direct response can be highly effective for certain kinds of products, of remarkable variety, from china collectibles through to elasticated-waistband trousers, and from dietary products to kitchen gadgets.

Direct response ads tend to give lots of information, provided in several styles within the one ad (lists of features and benefits, narrative descriptions of the product's appearance or provenance, and plenty of satisfied customer endorsements). They are, in effect, an entire marketing process rolled into one page or less: raising awareness, gaining attention, identifying needs, provoking desire, prompting decisive action. It is said that all would-be creatives in advertising should study the art of the direct response ad. So perhaps should we all, to better understand how marcomms is used at its grittiest.

HITTING THE TARGET WITH DIRECT MARKETING

Direct marketing or DM has much in common with advertising and is really advertising's sibling. The fundamental difference is that whilst advertising is, relatively speaking, a 'broadcast' activity in that the advertiser cannot pre-determine precisely who will see their message, DM is a highly-targeted (its advocates would say 'precision') activity. DM utilises market segmentation to a very fine degree and when used skillfully it can avoid much of the wastage of media spend which advertising suffers from.

DM refers to any form of marketing communication which can be aimed specifically at individuals about whom some prior profile information has been gathered. Its most common manifestation is direct mail (also, confusingly, known as DM) and now email marketing, but it can also embrace text and phone marketing, and even door to door approaches: providing that the activity is based on 'knowing' the target's profile and interests. So a mailing which you receive from a supermarket from whom you have a loyalty card, and which gives you specific offers based on your buying habits is properly called direct marketing, whilst a door drop from your local pizza takeaway is not. Similarly, an email you receive from Amazon which makes book suggestions based on your recent purchases is direct marketing, whilst random 'spam' mailings from companies you have never heard of are not.

DM's effectiveness depends fundamentally upon the quality of the data being used to identify and locate the particular profile of person that the advertiser wants to reach. The best data is acquired by companies 'organically' from their own customers. But there is also an entire support industry based around the creation and slicing up of data lists which can be purchased or rented by marketers for their campaigns. Many of the companies in this field are highly reputable and their data comes from people who have voluntarily signed-up to receive marketing information. But there are many less reputable providers too, whose data is culled from a variety of sources: often meaning that is unreliable or out of date, or that the people on the lists may not be willing recipients at all.

Its second challenge is to engage those people, which is far from easy for a number of reasons. Most notably there is the phenomenon of spam or junk mail which falls through everyone's letterbox on a weekly or daily basis. Good DM is quite different from junk mail. The former is highly targeted and tailored to the recipient, whilst the latter is blanket distribution of an email campaign which is not based on any detailed understanding of the interests of the recipients at all. Although quite different in intent and content, it is very easy for DM to get lost amongst the junk and to be tarred with the same 'bloody irritating' brush.

But another difficulty with achieving engagement in DM is the very fact that it does require some engagement on the part of the recipient: and this can be off-putting in itself. We can glance at a press ad or a TV commercial in our semi-conscious way, and we may still absorb something from it (the advertiser may still achieve part of their intended outcome). But for DM to work we generally have to do something: open it, hold it, turn it around or over, unpeel it and so on. It's for this reason that DM agencies (they are frequently, though not always, specialists in this field) produce ever more 'creative' solutions, particularly in business-to-business DM, where DM packs (as they are known) can be expensive and complicated items containing gifts and surprise special effects as well as text and imagery.

DM is a ruthlessly tested medium, and regular users of it (insurance companies are classic examples) are in almost permanent test mode, trying out subtle variants of content within the same campaign to see which have the most effect in sales terms with specific audiences.

PUBLIC RELATIONS: FROM GOODWILL TO PROMOTIONAL TOOL

Public Relations, commonly known as PR, has changed. Not overnight, but steadily, over three or four decades. Classical PR tended to be a 'corporate' activity, primarily concerned with managing the relationship between a company or organisation and all of its 'publics', but up until the 1970s this tended to be less concerned with pro-active promotion than with the reactive maintenance of reputation. The 'PR officer' from within an organisation, or the 'PR advisor' from outside were at their busiest at times of corporate development or indeed crisis: explaining to the media, to community representatives and indeed to Government and other authorities, why something had happened and what the company was going to do about it.

Whatever the topic or the audience, PR was much more about maintenance of reputation than about its creation. The old PR wasn't really part of the marketing field at all.

PR as we know it today is a very different discipline. It hasn't entirely abandoned its responsibilities as far as maintaining relationships between company and community (or company and Government, etc.), although it has passed much of that responsibility to those with the words Corporate Social Responsibility in their job titles. But it is now indisputably much more concerned with the active building of profile and the creation of reputation, and thus is much more intimately connected to advertising and other aspects of the marketing communications mix.

PR is really a collection of different disciplines.

Public Affairs is that element which maintains the traditional PR interests of positive relationships with a company's various publics, most particularly statutory authorities and Government, but also special interest groups and community representatives. Allied to Public Affairs is the highly specialist activity of *Lobbying* by which the company attempts to get its views and interests heard, understood, and ideally accepted, by decision makers in Government and other influential people and organisations.

Corporate Communications is closely related to Public Affairs, but is specifically concerned with outgoing communication activity by the company, including its annual reports, letters to shareholders, publications of various kinds, corporate video production for events and so on.

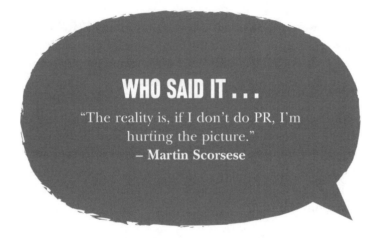

WHO SAID IT . . .

"The reality is, if I don't do PR, I'm hurting the picture."
– **Martin Scorsese**

MEDIA RELATIONS

For many the terms Public Relations and PR are synonymous with what is properly called Media Relations: the activity of gaining coverage of the company and its products in the press, on TV, on radio, and increasingly online.

Unlike advertising in which one has to pay for the media space, Media Relations works on the basis that the coverage has to be earned (by providing news of interest) rather than paid for. This is part of its great attraction, in that it is fundamentally a lower cost way to communicate than advertising, but it must be remembered that it has a substantial potential downside.

In advertising it can be said that whilst the advertiser is not necessarily in control of the output (the interpretation of the advertising made by the viewer or reader), they are at least in charge of the input (the advertiser is in complete control over what the ad or commercial looks like).

In Media Relations there is much less control of both input and output. Whilst the PR person will ensure that a press release and its accompanying photograph have been approved by the company, there is no guarantee that the submitted release will be used at all, and none that it will be used in its original form. Journalists will inevitably look for their own angle, and the resultant story may or may not paint a positive picture of the company. And even if the story is published verbatim, there is still no guarantee that the reader will interpret it as intended, or take from it the desired messages. Whilst it is true that people trust editorial more than they trust advertising, it is also the case that people are becoming increasingly wary of 'spin'.

For all its difficulties, Media Relations is a growing element of the marcomms mix, and is increasingly professional in its approach.

THE RISE AND RISE OF SPONSORSHIP

Sponsorship is conventionally bracketed under the PR function, but has become increasingly important, to the point where it is not just a discipline, but an industry in its own right.

Sponsorship has many attractions to the marketer. Depending on what is being sponsored it can allow a brand to borrow glamour or gravitas or some other desirable quality which might be absent from the company's intrinsic brand profile. A bank sponsoring an arts event or TV programme is a typical example.

It can give faceless corporate brands a populist touch and the opportunity for highly cost-effective brand awareness, such as with a giant insurance company sponsoring a major football team.

Success with sponsorship is must crucially dependent upon the appropriateness of the link between the two parties.

Sponsorship of TV programmes has become a popular alternative to straightforward TV advertising. Sponsorship 'idents' or 'bumpers' as they are known are short, branded 'mini commercials' which mark the start and end of TV programmes and of the commercial breaks within them. There are rules about the content of these 'idents', which prevent sponsors from overtly promoting product or brand. But far from limiting the desirability of these opportunities they are now amongst the most valued slots on commercial TV, and often show considerable creativity within the form, always aimed at building brand rather than direct sales. Sponsors have discovered a secondary benefit of the 'idents': they provide a handy stopping and starting point for viewers fast-forwarding through recorded programmes. An enviable place to occupy.

WHO SAID IT . . .

"Every sale has five basic obstacles: no need, no money, no hurry, no desire, no trust."
– Zig Ziglar

SALES PROMOTION

The reason I prefer to use the term Marketing Communications rather than Promotion when describing the whole topic of how a company speaks to its audiences is in part because it is important not to confuse the larger topic with one of its component activities: Sales Promotion.

Sales Promotion is concerned with adding value to a product or a service (usually on a time limited basis) in order to encourage purchase. Sales Promotion is so ubiquitous now, and as consumers we take its existence so much for granted, that we are surprised by its absence. Think of any visit to Boots the high street chemist, or to a CD and DVD store such as HMV, or a to bookstore like Waterstones. All three of these, and virtually every chain brand that you can name uses the 3 for 2 sales promotion technique virtually constantly: the variation being in which items fall within the promotion in any given period.

3 for 2 is a variant of the famous BOGOF (Buy One Get One Free) approach, but there are many different promotional approaches. Straightforward price reductions, multipacks, bonus (larger) packs, sample giveaways, points, coupons, on-pack promos (such as a free gift attached to a product), and competitions are all commonly seen in the high street and online. Another variant is the self-liquidating special offer, where items are sold at 'surprisingly' low prices if something else is purchased as well. Very common on petrol forecourts it is referred to as self-liquidating because no matter how cheap the item appears, it has cost the promoter less, and therefore the promotion pays for itself. Consumer promotions like all of these are most frequently funded by a manufac-

WHO YOU NEED TO KNOW
Robert M. Sandelman

He died aged 81 in 2009, a figure from a bygone age of marketing and sales, but Sandelman's influence is all around us. The inventor of the American Express Gold Card, the first charge card to be supplemented by customer rewards and privileges, Sandelman was one of the founding fathers of sales promotion. His central thesis was that it was more cost-effective to engage with customers directly through mailshots, vouchers, special offers, in-store demonstrations and sampling, and other non-advertising techniques, than it was to buy expensive space in the press and on TV. Sandelman believed the most important promotional outcome was to get the consumer into direct contact with the product, or its packaging, by the most direct route possible. 'Advertising,' said Sandelman, 'is a selling message in a medium the client rents. Sales promotion is a selling message in a medium the client owns – generally packaging.'

turer wishing to attract sales to their particular products, rather than by the retailer.

Sales promotion is common in the business to business market too, as part of the push marketing strategy, though it usually takes a different form. Often simple price cuts are offered which allow a bigger margin for the retailer, or in some cases the retailer will receive a fee for giving shelf space to a new product. Promotion can also take the form of financial or gift incentives to sales reps to encourage more active selling-in.

THE SURPRISING SURVIVAL OF THE SALES REPRESENTATIVE

Perhaps surprisingly given the complexity and sophistication of the marketing world, there is still a healthy role in the marcomms mix for the sales rep. Direct selling to consumers on the doorstep is far less common than in the past, so there are inevitably less sales reps 'on the road'. But the rep still plays a part, particularly in the business to business market.

It's easy to understand why. A company's business customers (to whom it wants to 'push') will be far fewer in number than its consumers, and they may be quite different from each other in profile and media consumption, which makes them much harder to reach cost-effectively through advertising or PR. Secondly, much business buying, because it is often more complex and protracted by its nature, revolves around a relationship of trust and service.

In these circumstances the sales rep therefore becomes a very valuable individual.

There are essentially two aspects to this kind of personal selling. Service selling is about sales made to existing customers. The job is to introduce new products, maintain and increase sales and margins, and to keep the customer satisfied. Development selling is about converting potential customers (prospects) into actual customers, which involves building the brand awareness, product knowledge and all the other elements of the marcomms process.

WHAT YOU NEED TO READ

▶ For a weekly insight into the advertising industry in all its creative splendour see *Campaign* magazine and its online home www.campaign-live.co.uk.

▶ For an introduction to 'the new PR' try Brian Solis and Deaidre Breakenridge's *Putting The Public Back in Public Relations: How social media is reinventing the aging business of PR*, FT Press, 2009, which apart from having a rather unwieldy title is gathering traction as being the best of the bunch of the so-called PR 2.0 books. Seth Godin said of this book: 'There will be two kinds of PR professionals in the future: those who read this book . . . and the unemployed'.

▶ *Advertising Age* both in its magazine form and online, is a very long-standing but still vibrant and vital window on to the world of American advertising. Contrast www.adage.com with the UK's Campaign site for a fascinating look at two parallel marketing cultures.

▶ Another, unavoidable, entry in the reading lists for Al Ries, this time with his daughter

Laura. *The Fall of Advertising and the Rise of PR*, Harper, 2004, has one central argument; that skillful PR will win out over advertising when it comes to effectively generating sales. It's a controversial position, and not everyone agrees with them (ad agencies most notably of course).

▶ As the Chartered Institute of Marketing is to the marketing industry generally, so the Chartered Institute of Public Relations is to the PR world. The CIPR is dedicated to professionalising the sometimes maligned 'spin' industry, and its website www.cipr.co.uk provides a very useful window on to the PR world as well as plenty of useful resources, and of course good filter for anyone looking for a reputable consultancy.

IF YOU ONLY REMEMBER ONE THING

The target audience for marketing communications is not just the customer who actually makes the purchase, but all the people who influence them.

CHAPTER 6

PRICE AND PLACE

WHAT IT'S ALL ABOUT

- ▶ Why distribution is a marketing function not just a logistical one

- ▶ The importance of the supply chain

- ▶ Why 'place' has changed

- ▶ Why 'price' is much more than just a financial equation

- ▶ Pricing strategies and tactics

Of McCarthy's famous 4Ps of the marketing mix, the least glamorous (and arguably the most neglected by otherwise enthusiastic marketers) are two and three: Place and Price. Yet without having your Product in the right Place and at the right Price, no amount of Promotion is going to achieve anything except frustration for customer and company alike.

GETTING IN FRONT OF THE CUSTOMER

At the opening of this book we considered an exchange, a barter to be precise, between two prehistoric cave-dwellers, one a skilled flint-knapper and the other a talented hunter. The hunter shared his kill in return for some sharp arrow or spear heads. It was a simple trade and not just because it did not involve any money: it was also simple because the 'supply chain' was very short, and very narrow. There were no intermediate players in other words, between the producer and the customer. In our example each cave dweller is actually both producer and customer, but that's not the point. The point is that back then, and for millennia afterwards, supply chains were for the most part very short indeed. Even at the point of history when farmers began to take their produce to a market some distance from their homestead, they would, for further centuries, often be selling their goods directly to customers who were also consumers of the produce.

The key to distribution (synonymous with Place in the 4Ps model) in that long gone era lay in the producer physically taking goods to a location where customers were likely to be found. Not necessarily easy of course, but certainly simple relative to most distribution in today's 'marketplace'.

We are now, as consumers, not only highly unlikely to meet the producer of what we consume (and this covers products and services or virtually every kind), let alone to haggle with them over price, but it is probable that most of us give barely a moment's thought, if any thought at all, to the origin of production of what we are buying.

There are some notable exceptions of course. Ethical, environmental, health and sometimes political concerns have prompted growing numbers of consumers to take an interest in the supply chain. The rise of the Freetrade brand, the fluctuating success of organic food produce, the measurement of 'food miles', and the current growth in the prevalence of farmers' markets are all examples of the market responding to consumer interest in the supply chain. The Governments of many nations, including the UK, have put substantial effort into persuading their consuming populations to buy home-produced goods. Remember the 'Buy British' campaigns? And there are examples in the service sector too: most obviously the popular resistance, frequently championed by sections of the media, to the off-shoring of services such as bank call centres.

Occasionally supply chain issues will make headlines. In recent years there have been popular anxieties over the reliability of gas supplies from Russia for example. And high-profile brands including Apple, Nike, Primark and many others have been criticised over labour practices in the developing world.

This list of exceptions notwithstanding, the broader truth is that the consumer and the customer alike are divorced from supply chain concerns: for most customer 'Place' simply refers to where they actually buy the product, whether that be on the High Street or online or elsewhere.

WHO YOU NEED TO KNOW
TESCO

Britain's biggest grocer, and second only to Wal-Mart in the table of the world's most profitable retailers, Tesco started life in 1919 as a market stall run by East End entrepreneur Jack Cohen, whose personal business motto, 'pile it high and sell it cheap', became one of the most famous mantras in business. Growing relentlessly through the economic and social changes of the twentieth century, Tesco adopted a consistent policy of acquiring smaller chains of stores and of constant innovation in customer service, from its pioneering Clubcard loyalty scheme in 1995 to becoming the first food retailer to make a success of internet shopping (with the slogan 'You shop, we drop.').

Under the energetic leadership of Terry Leahy since 1997, Tesco has continued to innovate, not only by creating huge (and hugely controversial) edge-of-town megastores, but by the creation of smaller 'convenience' stores under the sub-brands Tesco Metro and Tesco Express. The ubiquity of the Tesco brand (plus its alternatively branded One Stop chain) across the suburbs and in villages as well as in cities has caused a PR backlash, with the brand's iconic slogan 'Every Little Helps' amended by its opponents to 'Every Little Hurts'. But the company continues to post growing profits and is frequently cited as one of Britain's most trusted consumer brands.

THE MARKETER'S VIEW OF PLACE

For marketers however Place has much more complex implications. Place is concerned not just with the point of sale of the product but the steps along the way from production to that point, and of course all the players involved on that (literal and figurative) journey.

Part of the challenge of place for the marketer is that the concept is constantly in a state of flux, and never more so than today in the era of the digital revolution. Just reflect on how flexible the concept of place is now for customers and consumers. People can buy in malls, in High Street stores, on the Internet, from catalogues, and from all manner of combinations of these. Many shoppers will examine a product in a brick and mortar store before they buy online from someone else. Small retailers in particular often feel as though they provide free shop window and browsing facilities for their online competitors. And producers are of course constantly responding to this shifting notion of place. In the week that this chapter was being written The Sunday Times launched a new place for readers to access its 400 plus pages: and that place is actually another product from another company, the Apple iPad. The Sunday Times joins its daily sibling paper on the iPad, launched on the device in the summer of 2010. Like newspapers all over the world The Times group recognises that purchase of printed newspapers has been in decline for decades. The arrival of first the Internet, and most significantly larger format mobile devices such as the iPad give the product a whole new place in which to operate.

This example illustrates the point that place is no mere functional process (an unavoidable cost if you will) but is actually a key element contributing to the creation of 'opportunities for exchange'. The opportunity to exchange is the touchpoint between a producer's marketing offer and the customer's need or want. Without such opportunities there is obviously no marketing, indeed no trade at all. To put it another way, a great product, at a great price, and which potential customers recognise as meeting their needs, is still worthless without the place (actual or virtual) in which a purchase can take place.

In fact the smart marketer would go further and say that for a purchase to take place the product must not only be available in 'a' place, but must be in 'the' place where the customer is looking for it, or at least is likely to chance upon it. If it isn't there then the customer will likely buy something else instead, unless the product and brand are so distinctive as to be able to command the customer to invest effort and time in seeking it out.

THE SUPPLY CHAIN AND THE CHANNEL OF DISTRIBUTION

The terms supply chain and distribution channel are often used synonymously: but though related they

are not the same. The former described all the participants in the chain along which products pass on their
way from their point of origin to the final point of being
in the hands of the customer. With our cave dwellers the
supply chain was short as can be, with no intermediaries.
Similarly our small-holder taking produce to market.
Once the small-holder sells the produce to a shop-keeper
or market stall-holder the chain gets a little longer. Today
even the tiniest of home-based internet retail businesses
(e-tailing as it is rather clumsily becoming known) can
involve a substantially long supply chain. The e-tailer
may buy their products from anywhere on the planet,
and they may not buy from the producer directly, but
from an intermediary wholesaler. Then they need to
arrange shipping to their home or warehouse, then
onward shipping to the customer. Both shipping proc-
esses may also involve temporary warehousing. That's a
minimum of four links in the chain and probably more
(possibly stretching right around the world) for a tiny
business.

In this simple example the distribution channel and the
supply chain are virtually equivalent, but as soon as things
get a little more complex the differences between them
become clear, because the distribution channel describes
the path of the product through the supply chain.

If our imagined e-tailer not only supplies goods direct to
consumers, but also starts to supply a handful of other
retailers with the same goods, then the supply chain
starts to have breadth as well as length and instead of

one path or channel of distribution there are several. Even for small businesses things can quickly become complicated. And when one considers any business of size and even average complexity the picture can be quite difficult to chart let alone to describe verbally. Manufacturing companies for example can have supply chains of enormous length and breadth, with numerous possible distribution channels.

The precise form of the distribution channel depends upon the marketing objectives of the particular company: and that's fundamentally why distribution is a marketing concept not just a logistical one. An FMCG (fast moving consumer goods) company will want to get its products into all the branches of the major supermarkets (so its supply chain will have substantial width as well as length, with several complex distribution channels). A luxury apparel brand on the other hand will perhaps want to deliberately restrict its distribution to a small number of high-end boutique retailers, both to ensure high customer-service standards (not necessarily guaranteed even in expensive boutiques of course), and to maintain high price and demand by restricting supply. So this luxury company will have a much narrower supply chain with fewer distribution channels.

There is a very real way in which this whole supply/distribution thing can feel like it has nothing but downside for the marketer, and it is certainly true that there plenty of places for things to go wrong, and gaping opportunities for money to be wasted. The downside potential is obvious (loss, damage, time and resource required to manage the process, late delivery, disappointed customers, etc.). What is less obvious, but vital to the whole integrity of the supply chain process, and to its importance to marketers, is its potential to add value.

It's worth running through the key links in the chain, and as we do so to look out for the ways in which value is added.

MANUFACTURERS

Under this heading are included food producers and the creators of services of one sort or another. In fact of course there could be numerous links of the supply chain just under the single heading of manufacturer. A computer manufacturer actually relies on numerous other manufacturers to supply components (chips, batteries, etc.), and each of them relies on producers of raw materials or simpler component parts. All these manufacturers want to sell what they make and they all face two crucial marketing questions in trying to do so. First, what should they make in order to meet the needs of their potential customers? Second, how can they add sufficient value to the supply chain in order to win their place in it? The two questions are really aspects of the same one: so the component manufacturer adds value by adapting its technology, materials and skills to create the precisely specified component of the product manufacturer at the next stage of the supply chain (all at a price and service level which makes it more appealing for their customer to buy from them than to set up an in-house component plant).

WHO SAID IT . . .

"I love to go shopping. I love to freak out salespeople. They ask me if they can help me, and I say, 'Have you got anything I'd like?' Then they ask me what size I need, and I say, 'Extra Medium.'"
– Stephen Wright

RETAILERS AND RESELLERS

Although manufacturers as described above sell on to each other along the chain, they are not retailers. Rather retailers are those businesses who buy finished products and hold it in stock and put their efforts into selling it on to customers (some of whom are also end-users/consumers). Retailers come in many shapes and sizes, and of course operate in all kinds of different 'places'. Perhaps the big single marketing question for retailers to answer is what products to stock and in what quantities. The value added by retailers is fundamentally to provide the interface with the customer base: an interface which includes attractive displays and shopping environment, the opportunity for in-store promotion, the store's own advertising and so on. Without retailers in the chain manufacturers would in most cases have to deal direct with customers: to become retailers themselves. There are many large companies who do precisely that and manage to sustain large networks of stores which place themselves directly in the path of customers, but though their brands are high-profile and instantly recognisable and their value huge, they are vastly outnumbered by the hordes of manufacturers and retailers who work symbiotically together, concentrating on one role or the other, rather than trying to play both.

Resellers might be described as retailers within the business to business sector. Resellers purchase products from manufacturers and sell them on to business end users. A classic difference with resellers though is that they often add value in a different way, for example by matching a computer with specific software, or with other hardware (printers and peripherals) to create a 'solution' tailored towards the needs of a particular market segment.

WHO YOU NEED TO KNOW
Jeff Bezos

The founder of Amazon.com, the world's largest internet retailer, Bezos can take much of the credit (or blame, depending upon your point of view) for conditioning the world's consumers to buying almost anything online. Amazon sold its first book online in 1995, but famously did not become profitable until 2001. Playing the (relatively) long game has served Amazon well: it survived the massacre of the early dot.com pioneers and has grown to become by far the best known and most profitable of all internet retailers, selling a vast array of goods both real and 'virtual'.

Sales of downloadable e-books on Amazon now outstrip those of hardback printed books, and the Amazon Kindle e-reader has transformed from being a novelty device to being a virtual must-have for the modern lover of reading. Bezos has

187

innovated throughout the company's growth, both in its product choice and in its distribution. Nearly half the sales on Amazon are derived from its Amazon Associates affiliate programme and other third-party sellers.

Amazon boasts of having a wider range of stock than any other store, with its fast turnaround shipping supported by an extensive network of 'fulfillment centers' across the USA, Europe, China and Japan.

WHOLESALERS

Wholesalers add value to the supply chain by purchasing finished products from manufacturers in relatively large quantities and then selling them on to retailers in smaller quantities. Without wholesalers in the chain retailers would have little choice but to deal directly with numerous manufacturers, and those manufacturers would have to sell their products in uneconomically small numbers to each retailer. So value added at this link is two-fold: breaking down large quantities into smaller, and simplifying the stock purchase process for the players further up and down the chain. This comfortable relationship is long-established and has become increasingly sophisticated, automated and efficient. It is also, however, in decline. Wholesalers are suffering as more and more retail companies grow into large groups (through mergers and acquisitions) with vastly increased buying strength and desire to maximise cost-efficiency. Once a critical mass is reached the big players can either cut out the middle man (wholesaler) and deal directly with the manufacturers, or use their buying power to drive down prices to a point which squeezes out the potential profit of the wholesaler.

AGENTS

Unlike retailers, resellers and wholesalers, agents don't buy the products that they sell, but instead earn commission or fees by representing other businesses in particular markets in which they have expertise, contacts and established relationships (wherein lies their potential to secure a sale and thus add value). The role of the agent is to broker sales on behalf of others. Advertising agencies are so called because originally they earned their living not from their creative ideas but from commission earned on the advertising space in newspapers which they in-effect sold to their clients. Ad agencies are generally remunerated today by client fees rather than commission, but the name has stuck. Estate agents however still function largely according to the commission model: acting on behalf of the vendor to broker a sale, and thus earning a percentage. Interestingly this model is beginning to break too: estate agents are increasingly offering fixed-fee (i.e. non-commission) services to vendors, whilst others are turning the whole model on its head by working for buyers (for a finder fee) rather than vendors.

LOGISTICS COMPANIES

The term logistics embraces a host of services from warehousing, to international freight forwarding, shipping from distribution centre to high street store, delivery to customers and so on, all of which sounds simply functional, but which on closer examination is also a value-adding part of the marketing process: or at least can be if treated that way. The large trucks which trail up and down the motorways carrying goods to and from warehouses and shops are frequently branded as though they belong to one large retailer or manufacturer or another, when the likelihood is that they are actually provided by contracted transport providers. And there is more to the potential value-add than the advertising value of heavily branded curtain-siders. Value can be added through offering tailored delivery to customers, dealing with customer enquiries and so on.

Highly efficient logistics also means less need to manufacture, buy and store large quantities of stock, and thus minimises the risk of retailers being left with hard to sell items when the market shifts. The retailers' ideal is to hold precisely the number of any particular item that can be sold in the next hour, day or week. In most cases that ideal is unattainable, but the more sophisticated the logistics, the closer the retailer can get: not just cutting down on risk and waste, but providing faster response to changing fashions and giving customer more reason to re-visit a store more frequently.

THE POWER RELATIONSHIP BETWEEN PLAYERS

The relationship between the various players in the supply chain is theoretically of benefit to all, but it is often a tense relationship, in part because it is based on dissimilarities of power. The large supermarkets for example are famously more powerful than individual (and even collective) food producers and can thus dictate the quality and price of products, as well as demanding uniformity of size, shape and colour of vegetables and fruit (uniformity of farmed produce being expensive and difficult to achieve). And small brands wanting to get a foothold on shelf space are always at the wrong end of a power relationship with large retailers.

Those large supermarkets however are rather less power-ful (or at least might be said to be less bullish) in relation to the heritage brands which they have to stock (because their customers would be baffled if they weren't on the shelves). Kelloggs, Heinz, Nestlé and other brand groups are in a much stronger position when negotiating with supermarkets than smaller companies.

Sometimes the power derives less from financial muscle and distribution footprint, and more from perceptions of expertise of quality. Thus a well established and respected jewellery retailer will be selected as a stockist by high end jewellery brands. The concept of flocking applies inside the store in cases like this. One up market watch brand will want to be in the same store as other high end watch brands.

There is also sometimes power at play deriving from legislative or regulatory systems: most obviously in pharmaceuticals (certain drugs can only be bought from pharmacists, still others are only available with a doctor's prescription). But in areas relating to intellectual property of one sort or another, one player in the supply chain can gain a kind of power through a trademark for example.

Perhaps the greatest power of all comes from the building of a brand which is not only desired by the end customer, but known by others in the chain to be desired. Very few players anywhere in the supply chain of a world class brand will want to do anything but cooperate. Being in the chain of a famous brand (even with high pressure both to perform and simultaneously to keep costs ever lower) will be preferable to being out of the chain, partly because of the kudos achieved which in turn can attract other business.

CHOOSING THE MARKET 'PLACE'

At what might be called the sharp end of the supply chain is the place where company meets customer. Choosing where to make that engagement is as important a choice for the marketer as choosing the most advantageous place on the battlefield is to a military commander.

And it isn't just a logistical choice, or one of convenience, but one intimately linked with brand aspects of marketing. Choosing the 'place' is also an expression of 'brand positioning'. An up market restaurant is more likely to locate itself, for obvious reasons, in an affluent or stylish neighbourhood or city quarter. The location of physical shops and other outlets reflects the brand ambition of the business and will thus speak in some way to the prospective customer. Online the concept of the right neighbourhood doesn't apply. All websites are in one sense in the same neighbourhood as each other, and in another sense they exist in isolation. Online therefore the choice of 'place' is more to do with where the website is promoted or advertised, and it will be judged in part by the company its advertising keeps.

But there are also practical considerations to take into account about this aspect of place. Are the rents affordable? Does the location attract sufficient numbers of likely customers? One solution to the latter question is found in the phenomenon of 'flocking'. In any town one tends to find estate agents clustered together, often with solicitors nearby, similarly bars and nightclubs. Flocking can even extend to the point where a de facto branded location is created. Denmark Street in London is the nation's centre of musical instrument retailing. Theatre-land in the city's west end is, well, theatre-land. The key attraction of flocking is not only that of tapping imme-diately into an existing pool of ready customers, but the potential in the longer term of adding to the pull of the location for further customers.

TIME AND CONVENIENCE

It isn't really that many years since shops were generally closed in Britain on Sundays, the day of rest. It seems almost inconceivable now though that we shouldn't be free to go shopping every day, and virtually every hour of the week. The internet knows no time limitations and brick and mortar shops are fast learning to mimic it. Whilst high street shops are generally closed at night, neighbourhood convenience stores and larger out of town supermarkets are frequently open very late in the evening and in some cases 24 hours a day. Banking, holiday booking and any kind of shopping can be done online at any time, on any day of the year.

Decisions about opening times are in effect decisions about place or distribution: marketing decisions.

THE INTERNET IN THE SUPPLY CHAIN

It is virtually impossible to do justice to the impact of the internet on marketing in one whole book, let alone in one chapter. We address it in more detail in the final chapter. But it needs to be said in summary that the growth of the internet and digital data handling and communications has had a mould-breaking effect on almost every aspect of distribution. Consumers are now conditioned to expect and thus to demand huge choice and anytime access to purchasing opportunities. Buyers anywhere along the supply chain can source suppliers anywhere in the globe who can almost certainly be persuaded to compete on price with current suppliers. Suppliers can scour the web for potential customers.

Further, the internet allows producers of products and services, whether micro-local or mega-global, to touch end-customers directly, very quickly. Some discover that they can do business successfully with fewer or no intermediaries at all, shortening the supply chain almost back to medieval length. Doing away with as many intermediaries as possible is known as 'disintermediation'. But others will find that doing so actually limits their success potential, not least by alienating others in the chain that they can deftly circumnavigate in their early stage growth but whom they will later rely upon to build a larger business.

WHO SAID IT . . .

"The cynic knows the price of everything
and the value of nothing."
– **Oscar Wilde**

PRICING: NOT JUST A MATTER OF MONEY

Pricing, like Place, is frequently seen as a one-dimensional, functional, discipline. Often it is seen as a bit distasteful, vulgar or associated oddly with questionable ethics. Pricing conjures up questions of transparency, honesty, and morality.

A curious aspect of pricing is its dominance in the market place as a measure of value. We consumers have got so used to looking for bargains, offers, and 'best' prices, that we have learnt to equate lowest price with best value. No surprise then that most (though not all) producers and retailers tend to respond to our expectation by fulfilling it, focusing us even further on price with constant offers and other price-fixated strategies and tactics.

Another aspect of pricing to consider is that prices often appear to be set by looking down the wrong end of the telescope: instead of considering the market response to a price, there is a strong tendency to set price according to the cost of production. We will look at that tendency, and some other pricing approaches, in a little more detail.

CUSTOMER VALUE PRICING

The concept of customer value refers to the oft forgotten truth that it is not just the price on the swing-tag that is important to the customer, but the overall 'sacrifice' that they have to make to obtain the product. The real price equates to the financial price plus the time, plus the effort of obtaining the product, plus the sacrifice of all the other alternative uses to which the money, time and effort could have been put. True, most of the time the customer is not consciously thinking of these non-price-tag aspects. Most of the time. But they are there sure enough, in the equation, even if back of mind and unarticulated.

REVENUE AND PROFIT

In considering the role of Price it is also critical for any business to be clear about the difference between sales revenue and profit. They are frequently confused, especially by new businesses, and often by those large enough and mature enough to know better.

Sales revenue in any given period is easily calculated: it is the selling price of an item (whether of service or product, or indeed experience) multiplied by the number of sales in the period. You sell 1000 pies and at a price of £2.00 each and your sales revenue is £2,000.00.

But profit is a horse of a rather different colour. Profit equates to the sales revenue less the costs incurred. So if one sells the 1,000 pies at £2.00 and earns revenue of £2,000.00 then to be profitable the costs of doing the whole thing need to be less than £2,000.00. And the costs to be taken into consideration need to be the total costs (not just the costs of promotion and packaging for example, but also of wages, rent and so on). Bring in revenue equivalent to total cost and the business breaks even, bring in less and the business runs at a loss.

Blindingly simple, but it throws up enormous questions for the marketer. How can revenue be increased? By selling more (increasing volume) of course. But how does one create more sales? By spending more on promotion? Perhaps, but that also increases costs, which will add to wrong side of the equation if the pro-motional activity fails to increase sales volume. Maybe it is better instead to cut prices? But this has its own challenges. Lower prices means less revenue per sale. And substantially lower prices can mean selling at a loss, not to mention adversely affecting brand image (by going 'downmarket') which alienate some customers and thus lead to a decline in sales. It's all a potential nightmare.

The pricing challenge in a nutshell is to find the highest price at which the optimum number of items will be sold. And the broad principle behind that challenge is that of supply and demand, which says that price will fluctuate until it steadies and then settles at the place where it attracts sufficient buyers willing to purchase all (or most of) the goods that are available. In the real world this principle rarely works uninfluenced by other factors. There will always be, for example, cheeky companies willing to buy their way into a market by selling at minimum or zero profit, or even at a loss, and that approach will have a knock-on effect on prices in the sector and thus on other participants. Alternatively some companies keen to establish luxury or prestige credentials will be willing to sell at a very high price even though they may sell fewer items than they need to be profitable. In some cases there will be legislative caps on prices, as with utilities or bank charges for example.

PRICING STRATEGIES

A pricing strategy is a long-term approach to setting pricing, and is a critical part of the marketing process. There are two purposes behind having a coherent pricing strategy and only one of them is directly related to financials. First is the simple need, as described above, to achieve a profitable level of revenue. But second is a marketing or brand requirement, to use price as part of the narrative of the product: part of the image that it conjures up in the mind and heart of the customer.

Pricing can be used in this way to encourage trial amongst particular customer segments, to make a brand aspirational, to command loyalty, to revitalise a flagging brand or to introduce a new one, or to create a picture of 'value'.

MARKET-FOCUSED PRICING

A range of different approaches can be used to fulfill a pricing strategy, falling broadly into two approaches as outlined above: focusing either on the market or on the cost of production.

'Customer value' pricing prices the product according to what the customer is thought to be likely to be willing to pay, which in turn depends upon perceived value of the product.

'Psychological barrier' pricing sets prices at or just below what is thought to be the highest price to which the customer is willing to go for that class of product. Some classes of product are more inflexible than others in this regard. A paperback novel is unlikely, currently, to cost more than £10.00 in the UK (well actually it is more likely to be £9.99, for reasons which we shall come to presently). An appointment with a hairdresser might vary by a substantial factor, from £10 to £100.

'Going rate' pricing is related to psychological barrier pricing but focuses on what competitors are doing rather than on the customer. Retailers will huddle together, selling similar goods at broadly similar prices, nearly always keeping a price competition of a mild kind going, but generally speaking avoiding the temptation to dramatically undercut each other for fear of starting a destructive price war (and they almost always are destructive).

'Tender pricing' occurs in business-to-business, and most particularly in business-to-public-sector sales where different companies put in tenders, usually in secret, for a contract. If the right checks and balances are in place, and there are other factors considered as well as price, then this system can work effectively. But it has an unfortunate tendency to encourage under-bidding and sometimes what has become known as suicide-bidding, whereby a contractor will put in a bid so low that it is virtually guaranteed to win the tender but equally virtually guaranteed to fail to deliver on it. High profile contractor failures in the UK have illustrated this point in recent years.

COST-BASED PRICING

As the name makes clear, this approach takes the cost of production as its starting point. There are a number of variations on the theme.

'Mark-up' simply adds a fixed percentage, or other fixed amount on top of the direct cost of producing the item.

That mark-up is designed to cover all the other non-direct costs and to leave sufficient spare to make a profit. 'Full cost pricing' on the other hand starts by calculating real whole price of production and then add an amount on which represents profit. The problem with the latter method in particular is that the whole cost of production is extraordinarily difficult to calculate.

'Contribution pricing' takes the view that as long as sales revenue of an item contributes something towards the company then that is a positive. This approach might be used by a factory making a decision about whether to take on a contract which they would normally turn away as unprofitable but which can usefully use up spare capacity and thus make 'some contribution' to ameliorating the cost of maintaining the factory and its workforce. Equally a freelancer who charges a high daily rate might take on lower paying work in leaner times in order to avoid being unoccupied and unproductive. With product retailing this approach lies behind clearance sales: better to get something, no matter how little, for a sale than to throw the products away.

MORE PRICE COMPLEXITY

Most manufacturers make ranges of products (product lines) rather than just one item, and often those various products will have a complex relationship to one another. Car manufacturers, computer manufacturers, guitar makers, jewellers, household equipment manufacturers and so on, will make several models of various levels of prestige and size, and within each model range there are likely to be variants in equipment and finish, all building up to a complex tableau of prices in which the price of each individual item needs to make sense to the customer in the context of the whole range. Every price gives off a marketing message.

One of the most challenging (for the marketer) and potentially alienating (for the customer) approaches is 'discriminatory pricing' in which identical products or services are priced differently for different groups of customers. Commuters who have to use intercity train services at peak times will therefore pay substantially (often dramatically) more for their journey on an uncomfortably crowded train than a day-tripper travelling just a little later in the morning or earlier in the afternoon on a blissfully empty one. This delights the day-tripper and infuriates the commuter. All prices give a message!

Holiday accommodation is more expensive at school holiday times (discriminating against parents). Senior citizens travel more cheaply, as do young people and students. Those who can get to the bar for happy hour or to cinemas on a midweek afternoon get to drink or watch a movie less expensively. More enraging still to customers are discriminatory variants in insurance costs because of postcode: which to the individual car driver or home owner can seem to be acutely unfair. And perhaps the ultimate insult to a customer is the constant reminder in advertising by companies in various sectors that 'new customers' are entitled to savings and other incentives which existing customers are not.

All the approaches described above can be called strategic because they tend to be long term and go towards defining the company's brand position. But any company, at any time, is likely to experiment with setting prices tactically, which is to say to obtain a short-term effect.

PRICING TACTICS

Perhaps the most easily recognised and ubiquitous tactic is 'special offer pricing' which can include seasonal sales, new product promotions and other events. Offers can be highly effective and making substantial offers does not necessarily push a brand down market (after all, Selfridges has a famous sale), but there is a kind of etiquette surrounding special offers which relates to avoiding being too far out of sync with the rest of the market and doing what is expected and seen as reasonable. Which is why the 3 for 2 concept is so ubiquitous right across the retail sector from toiletries to literature. Nobody is threatened by it.

'Predatory pricing' by contrast tears up the rule book and tries to win sales and even to kill off competitors by selling below cost. It is actually illegal in the UK among other countries, but exceedingly difficult to prove.

Microsoft's effective destruction of Netscape by giving away Internet Explorer with every Windows software package is perhaps the most infamous case which could fall into the category of predatory pricing. It is not the same as running 'loss leaders' which can attract customers to a shop or restaurant by virtually giving away a product, or a pizza. A loss-leader is a perfectly legitimate tactic, but has its risks: the maths only works if the customer drawn in by the offer buys something else whilst they're there!

ELASTICITY OF DEMAND

Perhaps the key factor determining whether a particular pricing strategy or tactic will succeed or fail is the relative elasticity of demand of a particular product. A product is said to be 'price elastic' if when a retailer lowers prices the effect is for sales to increase. Hurrah! With price elastic products there's a sure fire way to increase revenue – put the price down (carefully, and monitor the results).

A 'price inelastic' product won't respond so well to price cutting. Put your prices down and you'll sell the same amount and just have less revenue to show for it. But don't despair: because if you can establish that a product is price inelastic then you can increase revenue by putting prices up. Raise your prices judiciously and your sales will stay the same but you'll be more profitable.

FEAR OF THE ROUND POUND

Finally on pricing, have you ever wondered why you hardly ever see round pound prices in retail? You are much more likely to see a £9.99 on a price tag than £10. And much more likely to see £14,995 in a car window than £15,000. The reason is simple, if rather silly. It's hard wired somewhere in our psychology that seems to read the £9.99 as much more than one penny cheaper than £10, and so on as you move up the value scale. We 'know' that the difference is fractional, but we 'respond' despite ourselves as though the difference was significant. And once the majority of retailers marks prices this way, everyone else has to follow. When it comes to shopping we have a terrible tendency to behave like sheep!

WHAT YOU NEED TO READ

▶ Tony Cram's *Smarter Pricing: How to capture more value in your market,* Financial Times/ Prentice Hall, 2005, is an approachable introduction to the 'art and science' of pricing management. Full of big brand case examples it also gives practical advice applicable to any kind and size of business. For a weightier approach to the topic try *Power Pricing: How managing price transforms the bottom line* by

Robert J. Dolan and Hermann Simon, Simon & Schuster, 1997.

▶ For a closer look at the extraordinary and significant Tesco story, two books give very different points of view. Andrew Simms' *Tescopoly: How one shop came out on top and why it matters*, Constable, 2007, makes its position clear right from cover artwork featuring devil's horns as part of the Tesco logo. Read alongside Clive Humby's *Scoring Points: how tesco continues to win customer loyalty*, Kogan Page, 2008, which looks closely at the brand's mastery of Customer Relationship Management.

▶ To dive into the complex world of supply chain management and logistics visit the online home of the industry's professional body in the UK, the Chartered Institute of Logistics and Transport www.ciltuk.org.uk

▶ There are numerous books on the subject of distribution management and supply chain management. Julian Dent's *Distribution Channels: understanding and managing channels to market*, Kogan Page, 2008, sets out to explain clearly and in detail, how the whole process and the complex relationships within it are best managed.

IF YOU ONLY REMEMBER ONE THING

The power of price and place is not just transactional, it has as much power to influence business success as product and promotion.

CHAPTER 7

STRATEGY, PLANNING AND TACTICS

WHAT IT'S ALL ABOUT

▶ Marketing orientation and its alternatives

▶ Why a marketing orientation can cause conflicts

▶ The difference between strategy, planning and tactics

▶ The importance of a marketing strategy with constant feedback

Having looked at marketing from a number of different angles in the earlier chapters, we now approach two of the toughest marketing challenges of all. The first is the somewhat philosophical question of whether or not it is right for a company to be 'led by' marketing. The second is the nitty gritty challenge of putting all the elements of marketing together to create an implementable plan.

CHOOSING A STRATEGIC ORIENTATION

Philip Kotler, amongst others, says that any given business has four possible 'strategic orientations' to choose from. Three of the four begin with a particular assumption about what customers/consumers will want to buy, and more importantly 'why' they will buy. The fourth avoids that assumption by starting from a different place.

PRODUCTION ORIENTATION

Production oriented companies take the view that success lies in efficiencies of production and distribution leading to cheaper and more readily available products. New products are most likely to be versions of what they already produce, or alternatives which can be made easily using their existing production facilities. The thinking is that if one can get the product into the hands of the customer faster, and more cheaply, then success will be assured. In some circumstances, where demand is high relative to availability of product then this philosophy can of course provide success. Every company needs to be production oriented sometimes. But this outlook can also lead to an over abundance of low-priced (and not very highly valued) product. In other words the ability to churn out *cheap stuff fast* is not always the way to success.

WHO SAID IT . . .

"Removing the faults in a stage-coach may produce a perfect stage-coach, but it is unlikely to produce the first motor car."
– Edward de Bono

PRODUCT ORIENTATION

Despite the similarity of name, this is a quite different world view. Product oriented businesses strive not to make more things faster and cheaper, but to make the best possible things: working always towards improvements in functionality, quality, user-friendliness, design and so on. It sounds like a noble endeavour, but it can lead in extremis to the development of apparently exciting projects which take so long that they are left behind by technological developments or by shifts in public taste, or by economic change, or which simply do not have the persuasive appeal to the customer which its passionate creators anticipated.

SALES ORIENTATION

The sales oriented world view considers that the business challenge lies, at its heart, in persuading (by advertising, by promotional activities, by face to face sales) the potential customer to make the purchase. Sales orientation is not fundamentally about the product, or the customer, but about the transaction. That doesn't make the sales approach an invalid one of course, but it certainly makes it one that is quite different from, and narrower in its scope, than the last orientation option of the four: marketing.

MARKETING ORIENTATION

The marketing oriented business starts by trying to get inside the head and heart of prospective customers, focusing on an understanding of their needs and wants. The route to success therefore is to respond to those needs and wants, rather than simply to make cheaper things, or even better things, or to 'get out there' and sell anything that's in the warehouse.

WHO SAID IT . . .

"Our plan is to lead the public rather than ask them what products they want. The public does not know what is possible, but we do. So instead of doing a lot of market research, we refine our thinking on a product and its use and try to create a market for it by educating and communicating with the public."
– Akio Morita

So by this definition, is Apple a marketing oriented company? Is Ford? Is McDonald's? All of them spend huge sums of money on advertising: which superficially might indicate a sales orientation. All of them are constantly developing new, and 'better' products, which could be indicative of product orientation. Sony's Morita clearly said his company knows better than his customers and therefore knew better what products to produce for them. And all of them are concerned in one way or another with delivering a product that is 'affordable' (affordability being a relative concept defined by the customer rather than the company), which might be indicative of production orientation. So far, so conflicting.

But all four of these companies actually are utterly marketing oriented, as are virtually all the most successful companies of the modern era, whether large or small. And they can be described as such because whatever other considerations they have along the way, they always start from, and constantly refer back to, the needs/wants of the customer and the market.

Steve Jobs is often quoted as saying that he doesn't want Apple to be right at the leading edge of technological development, but just behind it, from which vantage point the market's desires can be best observed and responded to. Apple's success is not about technology for its own sake but about the creation and then meeting of customer desire through technology.

Four orientation strategies

START	FOCUS	METHOD	END

Production orientation

Factory	Low cost	Delivery to market	Satisfy demand

Product orientation

Design office	Product improvement	Prove benefits	Chosen over inferiors

Sales orientation

Warehouse	Shift product	Promotion & sales	Sales turnover

Marketing orientation

Market	Customer needs & wants	Multi-faceted marketing strategy	Customer relationship

CONFLICTS PROMPTED BY THE MARKETING ORIENTATION

Given the evidence of the success of the marketing orientation and the potential dangers of the alternatives (and you don't have to look to big business to see those dangers, just to the numerous independent shops opened up, and shortly after closed down, in the side streets of any town), you might reasonably ask why any company would do otherwise than pursue the marketing option.

The answer is partly historic: marketing is fairly late on the scene. Our cave dwellers notwithstanding, the modern discipline of marketing matured some time after the importance of production, finance, management of workforce, advertising, promotion and sales, were established.

The more longstanding and sizeable a company, the more likely these non-marketing functional areas are to have, as it were, the big seats at the boardroom table, and thus the influence over the company's long-term strategy and day-to-day operations. As Kotler himself says: 'Many companies claim to practise the marketing concept but do not. They have the *forms* of marketing – such as a marketing director, product managers, marketing plans and marketing research – but this does not mean that they are *market-focused* and *customer-driven* companies.'

So with strong agendas already in place which have different priorities, the marketer has not only to look outwards to the customer, but also to establish internal relationships and an internal understanding (and appreciation) of what marketing exists to achieve for a business. And it's not just a theoretical understanding that's required, but an embedding of the marketing-orientation in everything that a business does. You could say that crucial audience number one for the Marketing Director lives not 'out there' in the market place, but in the boardroom and the offices of all the functional heads of the business.

WHO YOU NEED TO KNOW
Theodore Levitt

Levitt, who died in 2006 aged 81 was a professor at Harvard Business School and editor of the Harvard Business Review. Famously credited with popularising the term globalisation, Levitt also has numerous powerful lessons for marketers. His definition of corporate purpose, to create and keep a customer rather than merely to make money, echoes Kotler's customer relationship focus. In his acclaimed and influential article *Marketing Myopia* in Harvard Business Review he urged all companies to ask the question 'what business are we in?'

Levitt's point was that most companies view their business from the perspective of the products they already make, rather than from that of the customer wanting to solve a problem. In his most frequently quoted example Levitt wrote, in regard to a DIY tool manufacturer's market: 'People don't want to buy a quarter-inch drill. They want a quarter-inch hole.' Regarded by many as a critical turning point in the history of marketing, Levitt's article emboldened marketers everywhere to see themselves as having strategic influence on their companies.

MARKETING STRATEGY TO MARKETING PLAN

It follows from the points made above that most marketing plans form a part of a wider strategic plan for a company or organisation. The marketing plan is always a response to the strategic goals of the organisation, and the marketing response will be made alongside other function plans. In the simplest of organisations the planning hierarchy will look something like this.

Hierarchy of planning

In a more complex organisation, one with a number of brands in its portfolio, the hierarchy will likewise be more complex, with finance, operations, HR and marketing (and other) plans for each brand. Although referred to as a hierarchy, implying a top-down flow of power and information, the higher plans cannot be sensibly embarked upon at all without a constant flow of information going upwards.

CREATING THE MARKETING PLAN

There is frequent confusion (not just in marketing but throughout business) about the difference between strategy and planning. Some say strategy defines the plan for the longer term, so that the difference between the two terms is simply one of time-scale. It always seems more helpful to me to think of strategy and planning as qualitatively, rather than just quantitatively, different. In other words to think of strategy as the setting of major goals.

Planning therefore, instead of merely being just like strategy but sooner, becomes more important in its own right: it becomes the examination and explanation of how we are going to achieve those strategic goals.

Finally, under this approach to defining things, 'tactics' or 'implementation' become the particular aspects of a plan which will ensure the achievement of the plan.

This gives us a view of strategy and planning in a general sense but we now need to define the special characteristics of a marketing strategy and plan. In Malcolm McDonald's thorough but approachable book *Marketing Plans: How To Prepare Them, How To Use Them*, the author outlines six purposes of marketing, which provide a very helpful way of looking at marketing planning itself. Marketing, says McDonald, is a process which allows a company to:

- ▶ define its markets;
- ▶ quantify the needs of groups (segments) within those markets;
- ▶ determine the 'value propositions' that are required in order to meet those needs;
- ▶ get everybody in the company to understand, appreciate and 'buy in' to their particular role in delivering those value propositions;
- ▶ deliver on the communications elements of the propositions (note that the marketing function is delivering on the communications aspects, whilst other aspects have therefore to be deliv-

Marketing strategy, planning and tactics

MARKETING STRATEGY: SETTING THE MAJOR MARKETING GOALS

MARKETING PLANNING: STEPS TO ACHIEVE MARKETING GOALS

MARKETING TACTICS/IMPLEMENTATION: ACTIONS TO ACHIEVE PLANNED STEPS

ered by others in the company: therefore by definition marketing is a team effort across the organisation);

▶ monitor the value delivered by the whole process.

Understanding those purposes helps to clarify that marketing planning is a process which is not linear but iterative, and requiring constant feedback. But what does a marketing plan actually contain?

The four-step APIC model says simply that a marketing plan takes the company through a process of Analysis, Planning, Implementation and Control. But to really get a grip on what goes into a marketing plan the following five-step model can be more helpful. Note the two levels of feedback loop, influencing the tactical implementation, and the setting of strategic objectives. Each of the stages requires a more in-depth explanation.

ANALYSIS OF CURRENT SITUATION

Earlier in this book we have looked at a number of approaches to analysing the current situation, including PRESTCOM and Porter's five forces. Other sources of analysis include the Product Life Cycle (and its big brother the Market Life Cycle) and portfolio analysis techniques such as the Boston Matrix. A comprehensive analytical approach which looks at continuous data

Five step marketing planning process

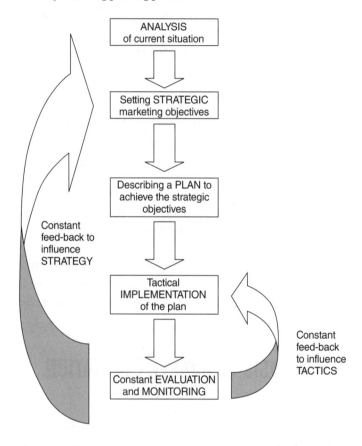

streams from both inside and outside the organisation, as well as considering market research and ad hoc collection of information, is referred to as a 'Marketing Information System' (MkIS). The idea of an MkIS is not just to provide constant information, but to turn that information into insight which can very rapidly (even instantly) influence marketing decisions at a tactical and strategic level.

Overall the analytical stage is asking the first of three key questions posed by Theodore Levitt in 1960 when he first described his concept of 'business mission': what business are we in, what business should we be in, and what business can we be in? The analytical stage is about the business we are in, as of now.

SETTING STRATEGIC MARKETING OBJECTIVES

The setting of strategy, by looking at goals, includes Levitt's second two questions: what should we be doing, and what do we have the potential to do? The setting of objectives, in order to be meaningful, has to be a rational activity, concerned with outcomes which we are not only able to describe before they occur but also to recognise as having either occurred successfully or failed, or occurred in part.

The popular mnemonic for that outlook is SMART (objectives should be specific, measurable, achievable, relevant and timed), and it is a guide which functions just as well in marketing as in any other aspect of business.

But that is not to say that a marketing strategy is limited to the mundane. Far from it. A strategy can be bold and evocative, describing the marketing philosophy and outlook of a company and the values that will guide its behaviour, as well as defining its ambitions.

Perhaps ideally a marketing strategy needs to be both philosophical and detailed. A well known high-end clothing brand set itself the marketing mission: 'dress the powerful'. In those three words an ambition is declared which is both general and specific (it defines a market segment with admirable succinctness). Beneath that statement though, evocative as it doubtless is to the company, must lie a more detailed strategy defining countries and regions, specifying more precisely who 'the powerful' are, and providing specific targets in terms of sales and/or market share, timescales and so on.

The strategic process includes the evaluation and selection of target segments, as well as brand issues including clarifying the differentiated positioning of the brand.

The strategic stage also involves some critical decisions about business direction, what Porter called Generic Strategies. According to Porter all businesses have to choose between one of three Generic Strategies: differentiation, cost-leadership, and focus.

Differentiation refers here to the idea of being highly distinguishable from competing companies by virtue of some competitive advantage (a better product in some way, or a more appealing brand for example). Often real differentiation will offer the opportunity to charge a price premium, or will increase the likelihood of repeat purchase, and so on.

Cost-leadership is not concerned with competitive advantage in the market place but with the producer achieving a lower cost-base (in production, distribution, etc.) which in turn generates higher profit margins.

Focus is about choosing to concentrate on a niche within a market and by applying all efforts to that niche achieving superiority within it. The niche might be geographical, or it might be based on a sliver of a market segment, based on customer profile.

Porter stresses that it is impossible for any one company, at any one time, to pursue more than one of these Generic Strategies. The result of trying to do so he says, will be muddle, confusion and dilution of the marketing effort.

WHO YOU NEED TO KNOW
Igor Ansoff

Known as the father of Strategic Management,
Ansoff, who was born in Vladivostok, Russia
in 1918, in effect gave companies and
organisations a methodology by which they
could plan for and make decisions about their
future. Prior to Ansoff's hugely important book
Corporate Strategy business planning was limited
in the main to budgetary planning which
made assumptions about how a company would
develop with little regard to the potential
and likelihood of the influence of change in
the external world.

Part of his crucial insight was that organisations
have a tendency not to understand the difference
between decisions that require fresh thinking,
and those which can be made through much
simpler policies: the distinguishing factor

being whether the situation is a recognisable one or a genuinely new and different one.

A keen advocate of detailed analysis of strategic situations, Ansoff nevertheless recognised that action could not be delayed forever and himself coined the phrase 'paralysis by analysis' to warn against the dangers of prevarication.

DESCRIBING THE MARKETING PLAN

The marketing plan now takes the ambitions of the strategy and applies minds to their achievement. What will actually be done to achieve the declared marketing strategy. But it must be remembered always that this is not just a question of advertising campaigns and other promotional activities. No, in fact it covers all four elements of the marketing mix, the 4Ps: Product, Price, Place and finally Promotion. It is this important point which gives marketing its strategic power and its potential (if addressed properly) to be such a critical influence on the fortunes of a business. Because as Kotler constantly reminds us, marketing is not about finding ways to sell the things we have made, but of achieving profit through providing customer value. So the marketing 'plan' is just as likely to make recommendations about what product or service must be provided, and at what price, and by what means of distribution, as it is to say how to promote it.

One helpful model for anyone involved in the planning stage is the Ansoff matrix, devised by business strategist Igor Ansoff. Properly called the Product-Market Growth Matrix, Ansoff's model gives the marketer four conceptual areas in which to operate.

The planning stage includes the critical discipline of setting a marketing budget: which is probably a greater challenge in the second decade of the twenty-first century than it has ever been before in the history of marketing. Marketers are obliged to prove (or at least give persuasive evidence of) Return On Investment (ROI), which is famously difficult to achieve. Increasingly, marketing oriented businesses are looking to customers to provide that evidence: not just relying on what customers say when asked, but in how they actually behave, based on measures such as customer acquisition, customer retention and the lifetime value of customer (an assessment of

The Ansoff matrix

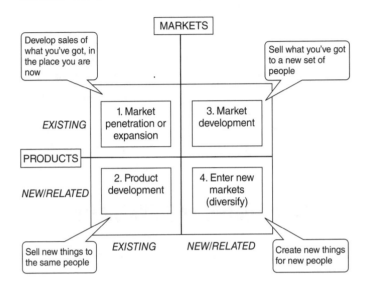

the overall spend of the customer with the company over the whole length of the relationship). As numerous companies will recognise, and some will admit, customers can be hemorrhaged from one end of a business just as quickly as they are recruited at the other.

At every stage the purpose of planning is not to be rigid but in fact to be ready for constant change in the marketplace and to ensure that others across the business become supportively involved in the marketing orientation of the organisation.

IMPLEMENTATION

We shan't dwell on implementation here, except to stress that it is in implementation that success can be genuinely achieved or go disappointingly awry, in part because implementation inevitably involves third parties (from advertising agencies and PR consultancies through to graphic designers and many more). It is thus at this stage when strategy and plan become the reliable guides to action.

MONITORING AND EVALUATION

The act of monitoring and evaluation, or marketing control as it is also known, is not the end of the process of course but the beginning of the circular feedback loop. Monitoring will look at the effectiveness of tactics undertaken, any shortcomings in the implementation, and changes in the market itself. All of these factors and more will then influence further implementation of the plan. The feedback loop is not only critical in actually honing and improving the marketing effort, but in keeping the rest of the company on board with that effort.

WHAT YOU NEED TO READ

▶ Igor Ansoff's *Corporate Strategy*, Business Library, 1988, first appeared in the 1960s but its influence is still felt and for some businesses its lessons will still seem revelatory.

▶ Theodore Levitt's articles are numerous, and all worthy of attention, and the best of them, including the legendary *Marketing Myopia* are contained in the collection *Ted Levitt on Marketing*, Harvard, 2006.

▶ Perhaps the most accessible contemporary writer on marketing planning, with a pragmatic approach which even includes a cartoon strip version of his work, is Malcolm McDonald. His books, including *Malcolm McDonald on Marketing Planning*, Kogan Page, 2007, and *Marketing Plans: How to prepare them, how to use them*, Heinemann, 1999, are very popular with working managers, and the innovative cartoon-based *Marketing Plan In Colour*, Butterworth-Heinemann, 2000, is a bold introduction aimed at marketers in SMEs.

▶ To dive straight into trying to develop a marketing plan for a business, the Chartered

Institute of Marketing offer a useful and free (though not altogether easy to use and save) online marketing planning tool: www.cim.co.uk/marketingplanningtool/.

IF YOU ONLY REMEMBER ONE THING

Marketing can only be truly effective if the organisation first gives a strong foundation to all its strategic decisions by choosing a 'marketing-orientation'.

CHAPTER 8

THE THIRD AGE OF MARKETING

WHAT IT'S ALL ABOUT

▶ Responding to customers' values as well as desires

▶ Why search has changed everything

▶ Horizontal, worldwide conversations

▶ A new agenda for marketing-oriented companies

Marketing has become established, highly influential, and in many senses settled in its ways. As it has gained in confidence and scope marketing has produced a vast body of theoretical work, research, and a hugely extensive popular literature.

FROM MASS MARKETING TO POSITIONING, TO LOVE!

As the age of mass production and mass marketing came to an end, so marketing shifted focus towards the customer. Al Ries pioneered the concept of finding a 'position' in the mind of the consumer, helping to open the door for a new mind-set in which the customer was firmly at the centre of things.

It was a dramatic shift in perspective. The idea that business should no longer focus on what it wanted to make and sell but instead on what the consumer wanted to buy was (at least within the confines of business and the consumer economy) radical and massively significant. The shift not only forced big companies to rethink everything about how they did business, but it also changed what consumers thought about their own role.

In the mass-marketing era the consumer had been a passive recipient of big company messages and the eager buyer of products which we were told would make our lives more comfortable, more fun, more glamorous and more 'modern'.

In the second age, by contrast, consumers were no longer seen just as open mouths and wallets, but the new commanders of what was produced and sold. In that new age of consumer-focus the new discipline of market research grew in importance. Every company wanted to know what consumers thought and felt, how they behaved, and how they were likely to respond to new products and messages.

WHO SAID IT . . .

"The illiterate of the 21st century will not be those who cannot read and write, but those who cannot learn, unlearn and relearn."
– **Alvin Toffler**

And in that second age, when marketing itself really grew up as a discipline, marketers became concerned not only with the head but with the heart. Some would call that era, from the early 1970s onwards, the great age of 'brand-marketing'. It started with the head (positioning) but it became clear, as we came to understand that purchasing decisions were in fact highly emotional, that an advantageous 'position' was no longer sufficient to win customers over.

So vast fortunes were spent by marketers over the last three decades of the twentieth century on exploring and attempting to refine better and better ways of winning customers' interest and loyalty. Marketing became engaged increasingly in mastering the elusive art of forming and maintaining 'relationships' with customers.

Eventually the notion of relationship morphed into something analogous to a love-affair or even a marriage. Kevin Roberts devised the elegantly intoxicating Lovemarks model in the opening years of the new Millennium, focusing unashamedly on emotion to win 'loyalty beyond reason'.

Of course these shifts in marketing focus were not happening in an unchanging world but one in which the pace of change was accelerating faster than ever. So dramatic and so rapid have been the technological, political and economic changes of the last decade of the twentieth century and the first decade of the 21st, that marketing can be seen running breathlessly to keep up.

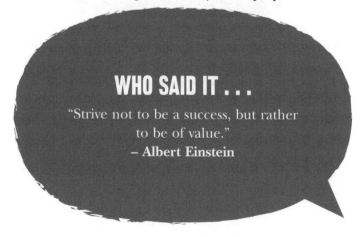

WHO SAID IT . . .

"Strive not to be a success, but rather to be of value."
– **Albert Einstein**

THE DAWN OF MARKETING 3.0

That is not to say that the concepts of Lovemarks, and brand, and positioning, and the 4Ps, and all the other marketing concepts covered in this book have suddenly become irrelevant: far from it. But what is certainly true is that they are no longer adequate alone, and they can help us now only if seen within the context of the arrival of a new age of marketing.

In his book *Marketing 3.0* the ever watchful Philip Kotler (who has lived and advised through so many years of marketing change) describes this new era as one in which marketers must look to the fulfillment of the human spirit.

But what does this so-called Marketing 3.0 actually mean in practice and why is it so important? The short answer is that it sets a new agenda. If the first age of marketing was concerned with satisfying *material* needs and wants, and the second age focused on *emotional* satisfaction, then the third age can be described as having as its key focus the meeting of needs derived from *values*. It's an even more remarkable and significant shift than the one from product-focus to customer-focus, and more remarkable still for the speed at which it has happened and the way in which it has taken all of business, and society, by surprise.

The origins of Marketing 3.0, just like those of its predecessors, lie in technology, and specifically the rise of digital technology. In a general sense one can say that the second age of marketing (the 'information' age as it is also known) closely correlates to the rise of the personal computer and the birth of the Internet. In fact the second age of marketing could not have matured without the Internet. It is the Internet that allowed customers to get to the pinnacle of purchasing power represented by the plethora of price comparison sites, and the ability to buy online and from their home virtually any product or service. But the Internet alone could not have given rise to the third age of marketing. That required the next turn of the digital wheel and the arrival of Web 2.0 with the participative potential that quickly led to the rise of social media.

THE ARRIVAL OF THE GLOBAL CONVERSATION

By allowing anyone on the planet who could access a computer and the internet to contribute original content easily and instantly, Web 2.0 began a global conversation. From MySpace and Facebook, to YouTube and Twitter, and the hundreds of other communities and networks: this wasn't just a new development in the way people communicated but a cultural revolution, the real significance of which is only just beginning to be grasped by business.

The first instinct of marketers as the era of social media dawned was to call it 'new media' but actually to still see in terms of the old media: merely as a new channel by which the old marketing methods could be delivered to consumers. But social media, we know now, is of course much more than that because it changes the balance of power. By virtue of social media the hypothetical 'consumer' no longer has to rely either on marketing messages from companies, or indeed advice and opinions from experts.

In the age of social media, the age of the online conversation, the 'consumer' seeks opinion and guidance not from companies or experts but from peers, from members of their network or community. And it doesn't matter that these network members are actually strangers, nor that these strangers' values and lifestyles might be quite different from their own: what matters is simply that they are members of the network and prepared to engage in the conversation.

Think about the book and product reviews on Amazon. Or the hotel reviews on TripAdvisor. Or the reviews of virtually any product or service on forums all over the web. We don't have to take the company's word for anything anymore. We can (and do) ask other people.

The character of this online conversation can be shocking and frightening to the conventional marketer who has been used to devising creative and smart messages which cleverly second-guess the desires of the consumer. Suddenly marketers are faced with a vast and infinitely complex network of recalcitrant 'prosumers' (proactive rather than reactive in other words) who are no longer content to accept marketing messages at face value.

THREE DEMANDS OF THE NEWLY CONNECTED CONSUMERS

These newly connected 'rebel' consumers want something new from us: and it's not just new products. The demands of these rebels are threefold:

1. They demand to actually participate in creating products and services: not just to choose from the range that we give them. Henry Ford said the Model T buyer could have any colour they liked as long as it was black. The prosumer of the third age says they'll have the colour, the specification, and the price that they damn well want. They don't want to buy the world's biggest encyclopaedia, they want to write Wikipedia together!

2. They demand that their concerns and values be addressed just as much as their needs and personal wants. The consumer of the third age is in a sense doubly-selfish. They don't just demand great stuff: they also demand to buy it from a company that is making outstanding efforts to make the world a better place (addressing environmental, health, ethical and other 'political' concerns).

3. They demand that companies acknowledge that (or at least behave as if) the power relationship has changed, that the consumer network is now the equal of the businesses that once 'ruled over them'. To those companies that appear to comply with this power shift, the consumer will give his or her loyalty. This third element of the new relationship is a subtle one and easily misunderstood. Apple fans hang on every word of Steve Jobs' keynotes announcing new products. Jobs is a kind of hero: but that doesn't mean that his customers feel inferior. Far from it. The Apple customer and the company have a relationship of mutual respect. They know it. He knows it. It is a consumer-business relationship quite different in character from any conceivable in a previous marketing age.

Furthermore, the way in which the new consumers behave, in exercising their demands, is radically different from just a decade ago. Some disgruntled customers still write direct with complaints to the companies which have let them down: but far more will Tweet to their networks, or update their Facebook status to let all their friends know about which company has disappointed them. Still others will add comments to news stories and blogs all over the world. Not only have the rules of communication changed: but the speed of its happening has transformed. Today if a company lets down a customer significantly it is likely that thousands of networked customers will know about the incident before the company itself is aware that anything has happened. Which is why so many big companies now have teams of people trawling the Web looking for comments about their brand: often approaching those who have made negative comments to try to mend the relationship.

Perhaps the most creative new-media response to an unsatisfying customer experience, and one which is said to have cost the target company (United Airlines) millions of dollars in lost share value, is the *United Breaks Guitars* music video made by Canadian songwiter David Carroll and his band Sons of Maxwell. Carroll's expensive Taylor guitar was damaged during unloading from a United Airlines flight, and the songwriter claimed to have seen ground crew throwing instruments on to the tarmac. After months of fruitless complaining through conventional channels Carroll's band shot a music video about the incident. *United Breaks Guitars* was posted on YouTube in July 2009. It received 150,000 hits in the first day and five million by the middle of the following month. After one year it had been seen almost 10 million times. A public relations disaster for United, the event not only highlighted a breakdown in customer service but the stark fact that most companies simply don't know how to deal with this kind of social media onslaught.

So how should marketers respond to this new age with all its terrifying unknowns and new rules? Most importantly they need to accept the fact that the whole marketing environment has changed, inexorably. Huge numbers of businesses appear still to be in denial, or to be accepting only in part, that something has changed (on the superficial level that they now have new opportunities to deliver the same old messages). Secondly they need to attend to the technological, behavioural and values changes which are demanded of them by the new era.

Of course the arrival of the new age of marketing does not diminish the importance of the concepts of customer-focused era, but it does put them into a different perspective. Instead of just focusing on the rational (the position of the brand in the mind of the customer), or on the emotional (the 'relationship', the 'lovemark'), smart companies now incorporate these into a broader vision which also takes account of the new values-based consumer.

It is now a triumvirate of factors, which support and strengthen each other.

THE REBIRTH OF MISSION STATEMENTS

So the big challenge for the modern company is to find a strategic marketing-orientation which can draw on the three factors of mind, heart and values, and which can allow the company to enter and participate in the new global conversation: a conversation in which the relationships between consumer and producer are now horizontal and equal, rather than vertical and hierarchical.

For some companies that understanding has led to a renewed interest in corporate mission. The 'mission statement' of the 1990s fell from favour, rightly, because it was usually self-aggrandising, unhelpful, obscure and meaningless. Companies got into the habit of posting long-winded and generic mission statements on their websites, on the walls of their reception areas, and in their annual reports, to no great positive effect.

But for companies of the Marketing 3.0 era, the notion of mission (which is now more popularly referred to as 'purpose') has a renewed relevance. Identifying a 'purpose' which guides the whole business can be the tool by which the three points of the triangle are tied together.

To be relevant and useful a company's purpose has itself to fulfil three essential requirements. First it needs to be authentic to the company's actual values and reflective of its actual behaviour. Not phony in other words.

Second, it needs to be distinctive. It doesn't have to be unique, but it should certainly reflect something that is differentiated from other companies, which reflects the particular and specific contribution that the company will make to the world.

Third, the purpose needs to be both relevant and com-pelling: in other words it must have the capacity to engage the customer's emotions, thoughts and values.

In a sense the consideration and adoption of a core purpose is the new starting point for brands in the new era of marketing: the answer to the question (sometimes voiced by customers, sometimes not, but nevertheless there in the background): 'What is this company actually for, and how does it contribute?'

The new marketing era virtuous triangle, with purpose at its centre

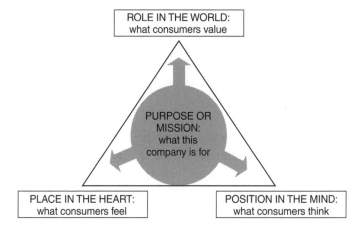

ROLE IN THE WORLD:
what consumers value

PURPOSE OR MISSION:
what this company is for

PLACE IN THE HEART:
what consumers feel

POSITION IN THE MIND:
what consumers think

POSITIVE ENGAGEMENT IN THE ONLINE CONVERSATION

Once a company has become properly aware of the new marketing landscape and addressed the need to adopt a compelling 'purpose', it then has to build the commitment to customer values into its behaviours. At all costs businesses must avoid accusations of 'greenwash' or 'fairtrade-wash' or 'organic-wash' or other suspicions that their values-based behaviours and policies are motivated by the desire for good PR. The tension between corporate behaviours that can win media Brownie points and genuinely values-led activity is a real one, and forms a part of the debate in the boardroom in which senior marketers might be expected to go one way (i.e. in favour of publicity wins) but should actually go the other way (i.e. in favour of strategic integrity). This is one of the ways in which the role of marketing has arguably become even more significant in the new era.

And once the values and purpose are in place? Then the big challenge for the modern marketing oriented company is actual engagement in the worldwide online conversation. There are countless books, articles and websites giving practical guidance on blogging, Tweeting, Search Engine Optimisation (SEO) and more. But far fewer address the strategic marketing issues around the online revolution.

To put the phenomenon at its simplest, the ability to 'search' online for virtually anything (a product, a service, a company, an opinion, a community, a network, a customer group) has completely moved the ground from under marketers' feet. It is not merely that a new medium has arrived: it is that the rules of marketing have changed as a result, and continue to change, fast and far.

In 2009 the number of online searches grew almost 50% over the previous year. Search is now the way by which the vast majority of web users enter the web.

WHO SAID IT . . .

"Searchers aren't an isolated demographic
from the rest of your target audience. Searchers
are your target audience. And they're telling
you exactly what will compel them to buy your
products, engage with your company, and
become your strongest advocates."
– Vanessa Fox

The term 'search' just refers to the simple act of typing
a word, a collection of words, or a phrase, or even a
complete sentence or a question, into the search box at
the top right of any web browser. When any of us type
the word or phrase and hit Enter or click on the little
magnifying glass icon a hugely complex process is initi-
ated, which is (astonishingly) completed in something
like 0.10 to 0.20 seconds. Tens of thousands, hundreds
of thousands (and frequently millions) of possible results
are returned to any given search, which either provide
us with the answer we require or (in the majority of cases
apparently) prompt us to refine or alter our search as we
home-in on the information we are seeking.

This not only matters to all marketing-oriented companies, but it matters hugely, and it matters in a subtly
different way from which most think that it matters.

SEARCH AS THE MOST EFFECTIVE FORM OF RESEARCH

Most importantly the search process matters to anyone concerned with marketing, not because we can throw ourselves into the tracks of any given search and shout 'Look at us, we've got something approximating to what you're looking for, so look no further' but rather because in the process of searching our potential customers are telling those who will listen something profound about themselves. The truly outstanding benefit of search to marketers therefore is not the ability to interrupt it (which is pretty much impossible actually, searchers will just ignore you and move on), but the ability to learn what it is that customers are looking for. In other words search gives marketers the cheapest and one of the most reliable means of researching a marketplace and consumer needs/wants/desires.

For small businesses which don't have big budgets for conventional market research, and for larger companies which want to listen with an open mind to customer wants and needs, search is an extraordinarily powerful tool. The major search engines (Google being by far the largest of course) all provide free-to-use tools which make analysing searches for any topic fast and effective. Companies huge and tiny alike are using Google's Keyword Tool to find out what terms people are actually using to find different kinds of products and services.

Analysis of search behaviour not only provides an insight into what customers are seeking, but it also gives clear feedback on the language that they use. Search shows that customers neither think nor use language in the way that marketers would imagine or perhaps prefer.

The most telling discovery is that searchers do not use the poetic or clever imagery and phrase-making of the advertising copywriter: they use collections of simple words and phrases to work their way towards their quarry. They often use those words non-sequentially, they often misspell them, and they use brand names instead of generic terms and vice versa. Most significantly of all, searchers work fast and furiously, and they are ruthlessly unimpressed by the attempts of marketers to catch them along the way: including by means of sponsored links (Pay Per Click advertisements).

One indication that companies have not yet caught on to the true character of searching is the fact that whilst nearly 90% of the money that companies spend on search is spent on Pay Per Click, some 85% of searches use only organic results (the so-called 'natural' listings). To put it another way searchers are, en masse, ignoring sponsored links on the web and are much more inclined to trust the natural listings. That's not to say that Pay Per Click advertising is redundant of course. Curiously it appears that natural listings which are supported by PPC links on the same page are trusted even more than those which appear alone: which gives marketers a double challenge (the sponsored links do matter and are worth investing in, but for the subtle reason of giving weight and further credence to a natural listing).

NOT SEARCH TACTICS BUT SEARCH STRATEGY

So you shouldn't be abandoning PPC: but what you should be doing (and most businesses are taking time to catch on to this), is devising a search strategy which is based around natural listing as the priority. As described above, there is much talk about tactics and techniques for trying to achieve 'high rankings' in search. The trouble with most of the popular 'fast track' ways to get your business higher up the natural listings is that their effectiveness is actually very limited. Such is the sophistication of the search engines that it is harder and harder to cheat one's way to the top. Some techniques will simply give disappointing results. Others will get your website banned by search engines completely, either temporarily or permanently, and still others will be seen for what they are by searchers (superficial and attention-grabbing behaviour) and thus will be ignored.

In fact there is no sure-fire *tactical* way to ensure that your website does well on the search engines: which underlines why companies need to adopt a *strategic* approach. A search strategy should, like the overall marketing strategy, ask fundamental questions about the business (what is our business for, why should it matter to our customer, what is our customer looking for, and does what we provide match the needs/wants/desires of the customer?).

From that strategic viewpoint a company can then not only build web content which matches the search interests of real customers, but can create and refine products and services which match those search interests too.

WHO YOU NEED TO KNOW
Gary Vaynerchuk, Brian Solis,
David Meerman Scott
Three Stars of the Social Media Scene

Gary Vaynerchuk is a sommelier who has been so successful at using social media to boost his family wine business (taking it to $50 million turnover) that he has become an acknowledged expert in the field, a hugely popular blogger and a bestselling author with *Crush It*, a guide to turning hobbies into businesses through the power of social media. Find him on Twitter @garyvee along with his extraordinary 856,000 followers.

Brian Solis is principal of the award winning silicon valley PR and new media agency FutureWorks and co-author of *Putting The Public Back in Public Relations*. Find him on Twitter @briansolis.

David Meerman Scott is a marketing strategist, master blogger and author of numerous books including *The New Rules of Marketing and PR* and its follow up *Inbound Marketing: Get Found Using Google, Social Media and Blogs*. Find him on Twitter @dmscott.

THE SEARCH CONVERSATION MINDSET

From that point onwards it is a matter of adopting a 'search conversation mindset' which will lead in turn to engaging effectively in online communities from Facebook to Twitter and beyond. But it always has to be remembered that it should be a conversation, not a sales pitch. Companies which try overtly to muscle in on the horizontal online conversation in order to sell will find repeatedly that their brand reputation suffers. Home-furnishing store Habitat bruised its own brand badly in 2009 by misusing Twitter's 'hashtag' system in order to elbow its way into conversations about completely unrelated topics: including, most infamously, serious news and discussions about the Iranian elections. The rules of the social media conversation are much like those of any conversation: joining in is a privilege rather than a right, and it's easy to look boorish if you're not genuinely in tune with others in the room.

Some brands though have become early exemplars of how to use media like Twitter highly effectively. Whole Foods Market, based in Austin, Texas, has a staggering 1.84 million followers on Twitter and nearly half a million 'likes' on Facebook. Followings like that come from providing a constant stream of valuable information, but also by actually engaging in a proper conversation: listening, answering questions, being genuinely interested as well as interesting.

And there are numerous examples of 'micropreneurs' using the new tools to make an impact way out of proportion to their size as businesses. You don't have to look far to see it happening either. In my home city of Norwich two makeup artist sisters Sam and Nicola Chapman have created a YouTube channel called Pixiwoo which offers cosmetic advice. This is two young people working from a home 'studio' on virtually no budget, but who have attracted nearly 200,000 channel subscribers and almost nine million views. There'll be examples in

your neighbourhood too: small businesses, entrepreneurs, individuals and communities, who have realised
the potential of the new technology. When large companies can make the same engagement we will know that
marketing has really adjusted itself to its third age.

There are so many possible platforms, with more arising
all the time, that a printed book like this one can never
be completely up to date with developments. But the
trend is clear. From the snowballing of Facebook (now
theoretically the world's third most populous country
and so important that it became the subject of a hit
Hollywood movie only six years after its creation), to the
appearance of scrapbook-style 're-bloggable' blogging
platforms like Tumblr the digital genie isn't going to go
back in the bottle.

In the end a proper strategic approach to search and to
social media will not only influence a company's online
activity and behaviour, which can lead to positive rewards
in terms of reputation, loyalty, customer engagement,
and ultimately sales, but it can and should influence the
company to constantly assess and adjust to meet the aspirations of its customers.

WHAT YOU NEED TO READ

▶ The most straightforward guide to the power of search is Vanessa Fox's *Marketing in the Age of Google*, John Wiley & Sons Ltd, 2010. Straddling strategic and tactical issues this book will be as enlightening for the board of many large companies as it will be practical for the heads of smaller ones.

▶ Philip Kotler again, this time with the assistance of Hermawan Kartajaya and Iwan Setiawan, has produced the first slim-volume strategic marketing overview of the new marketing age: *Marketing 3.0*, John Wiley & Sons Ltd, 2010.

▶ For an immediate plug-in to all the latest in 'future technology, culture and science' which is always at the leading edge of all things web oriented, dive into *Wired* in print as a monthly magazine but crucially online at www.wired.com/ (for the US version) and www.wired.co.uk/ for the British.

▶ For a direct hands-on experience of the power of search go to the ultimate (at least for the moment) source: www.google.com/ or

www.google.co.uk/, and once there do a
Google search for [google keyword tool]. Ten
minutes using this tool should persuade any
doubter about the significance of search.

IF YOU ONLY REMEMBER ONE THING

The new age of marketing is characterised by
horizontal online conversations between vast
numbers of people unlimited by geography or
demographics.

CONCLUSION

At the time of writing there is a huge buzz about 'mobile' marketing, reaching out to consumers on mobile devices from smart-phones to tablets such as the iPad. Within the coming months and few years there will inevitably be further technological developments. But what is as yet unproven is whether brands will simply use these opportunities as they come along just as new interruption channels or as exciting ways of genuinely interacting and engaging with audiences.

All of which brings us back to the beginning of this book and the notion that marketing is about providing customer value. The third era of marketing, with its combining of heart, mind and values, and this era's new digital environment, is the most exciting era to live and work in, giving marketers their greatest ever challenges in providing that value.

We marketers can no longer give people what *we* think that *they* want. Nor indeed can we just research what customers appear to want and then provide it.

Instead in the new era we must engage with customers as never before, and together with them create the things that we both want, whilst at the same time reflecting the values and concerns of our age. There's never been a more important or inspiring time to be a marketer.

ACKNOWLEDGEMENTS

Most importantly of all I have to acknowledge all the marketing experts, academics, practitioners and authors who have not only inspired and educated me, but whose expertise I have plundered over the past several months in the writing of this book. All the knowledge is theirs and any mistakes in the interpretation and telling of it are mine.

Thanks are due too to my clients in the UK and beyond who have given me wonderful opportunities to be involved with such stimulating marketing challenges over the years.

Thanks of course to the team at John Wiley: this series was a great idea and it was a thrill to be part of it. And special thanks to my agent Diane Banks.

Finally, huge thanks to my family for allowing me to shut my office door to stay hidden for hours on end, only to appear late in the evenings like a hungry, grouchy bear at the dawn of spring.

INDEX